my revision notes

WJEC GCSE

RELIGIOUS STUDIES

Unit 2 Religion and Ethical Themes

Joy White and Gavin Craigen

The Publishers would like to thank the following for permission to reproduce copyright material.

Photo credits
p.34 © Fotolia.

Acknowledgements

Translations of sacred texts
Quotations from the Bible: THE HOLY BIBLE, NEW INTERNATIONAL VERSION®, NIV® Copyright © 1973, 1978, 1984, 2011 by Biblica, Inc.® Used by permission. All rights reserved worldwide.

Quotations from the Qur'an: Sahih International translation © 2016 QURAN.COM. ALL RIGHTS RESERVED.

Every effort has been made to trace all copyright holders, but if any have been inadvertently overlooked, the Publishers will be pleased to make the necessary arrangements at the first opportunity.

Although every effort has been made to ensure that website addresses are correct at time of going to press, Hodder Education cannot be held responsible for the content of any website mentioned in this book. It is sometimes possible to find a relocated web page by typing in the address of the home page for a website in the URL window of your browser.

Hachette UK's policy is to use papers that are natural, renewable and recyclable products and made from wood grown in well-managed forests and other controlled sources. The logging and manufacturing processes are expected to conform to the environmental regulations of the country of origin.

Orders: please contact Hachette UK Distribution, Hely Hutchinson Centre, Milton Road, Didcot, Oxfordshire, OX11 7HH. Telephone: +44 (0)1235 827827. Email education@hachette.co.uk. Lines are open from 9 a.m. to 5 p.m., Monday to Friday. You can also order through our website: www.hoddereducation.co.uk

ISBN: 978 1 5104 2344 2

© Joy White and Gavin Craigen 2018

First published in 2018 by Hodder Education (a trading division of Hodder & Stoughton Limited), An Hachette UK Company
Carmelite House
50 Victoria Embankment
London EC4Y 0DZ

www.hoddereducation.co.uk

The authorised representative in the EEA is Hachette Ireland, 8 Castlecourt Centre, Dublin 15, D15 XTP3, Ireland (email: info@hbgi.ie)

Impression number   10 9 8 7 6
Year   2025

All rights reserved. Apart from any use permitted under UK copyright law, no part of this publication may be reproduced or transmitted in any form or by any means, electronic or mechanical, including photocopying and recording, or held within any information storage and retrieval system, without permission in writing from the publisher or under licence from the Copyright Licensing Agency Limited. Further details of such licences (for reprographic reproduction) may be obtained from the Copyright Licensing Agency Limited, www.cla.co.uk.

Cover photo © Leigh Prather/Shutterstock.com

Illustrations by Aptara Inc.

Typeset by Aptara Inc.

Printed and bound by CPI Group (UK) Ltd, Croydon, CR0 4YY

A catalogue record for this title is available from the British Library.

Introduction

Throughout this revision guide there are a number of features which will help you revise and also help you to answer the questions in the exam. Each feature is indicated by a logo.

> **Key concepts**
> In each unit you will study there will be at least eight key concepts which you must know. The first question of each unit will ask you for a definition of a key concept. Correct definitions gain 2 marks. It is also important to use the key concepts in b-, c- and d-type questions as credit is given for the use of religious and specialist language.

> **Explanation of key concept**
> As it says in the title, the concept is **key** (central) to an understanding of the religion or issue. It is important that, in addition to being able to state the meaning of the concept, you show an understanding of why and how that concept is central to the religion or issue. This information is particularly important for b-, c- and d-type questions.

In each unit an acrostic is used to show why there are differences of views and practices amongst believers of the same religion. Diversity comes from an assessment of the situation (S), teachings from that tradition (T), other sources of authority such as the Pope, rabbis (A), how those teachings are interpreted (I), e.g. non-literally or literally, and the role of conscience and reason (R). It is important in your answer to be able to explain why people of the same religion hold different views and beliefs.

| Reasons |
| Interpretations |
| Authorities |
| Teachings |
| Situation |

> **Activity**
> Activities are provided throughout the book in blue boxes like this one.

You will have very little time in your exam to answer some of the questions. It is important that you are able to quickly recall important facts. Whenever you see the five finger logo it means these are the five basic and central facts of that issue.

It is important before you begin revising the content that you know and understand how marks are awarded. As you will see from the marking grids on pages 85–87, marks are given for more than just knowing facts. In some questions you need to be able to explain, make links, justify, give different views. In all questions you need to use religious and specialist language. The exam tips and exam practice activities will help you develop these important skills.

> **Exam tips**
> Throughout each unit exam tips are included which help you understand how marks are awarded (and lost). Doing well in the exam isn't just about all you know, it also depends on how you answer the questions.

 This indicates an important point to remember.

My revision planner

Part A

Christianity
- 5 The big picture
- 7 Beliefs: the Bible
- 12 Beliefs: the afterlife
- 16 Practices: life's journey – sacraments and key acts of worship
- 20 Practices: special places

Judaism
- 23 The big picture
- 25 Beliefs: sacred texts
- 27 Beliefs: the Covenant
- 30 Practices: the use of sacred texts
- 34 Practices: Jewish identity

Islam
- 43 The big picture
- 45 Beliefs: prophethood (risalah – Qur'an 2:136)
- 48 Beliefs: afterlife (akhirah)
- 52 Practices: Muslim identity and ummah
- 57 Practices: festivals and commemorations

Part B Philosophical themes

Theme 1: Issues of relationships
- 60 The big picture
- 62 Relationships
- 69 Sexual relationships
- 71 Issues of equality: gender prejudice and discrimination

Theme 2: Issues of human rights
- 73 The big picture
- 74 Human rights and social justice
- 79 Prejudice and discrimination
- 82 Issues of wealth and poverty

85 Marking grids

Answers at www.hoddereducation.co.uk/myrevisionnotesdownloads

Christianity: core beliefs, teachings and practices

The big picture

Below is a summary of the key questions for this study of Christianity:
- What is the Bible?
- What are the different ways of interpreting biblical writing?
- How does the Bible relate to other forms of authority?
- What is the afterlife?
- What are the beliefs about resurrection, judgement, heaven and hell?
- What are the sacraments and key acts of worship?
- How important is the Eucharist/Communion to Christians?
- What are the different Christian interpretations of Eucharist/Communion?
- How do Christians prepare for confirmation?
- What is the significance of symbols and vows in a Christian religious wedding?
- What is the significance of a place of worship?
- What is the purpose of pilgrimage?

> **Exam tip**
>
> It is important to use terms from the religions you have studied in your answers to examination questions. You will need to be able to define the concepts in each theme. The first exam question, for 2 marks, asks for a definition of a concept. To gain 2 marks you need to be able to give two separate points or a developed point.

Key concepts

The Bible is the Christian sacred text believed by Christians to be revealed and/or inspired by God, made up of the Old and New Testaments.

Revelation is God making himself known to humankind; for instance, through the Bible.

Judgement is the belief that God will judge whether or not humans are worthy to enter the Kingdom of Heaven.

Baptism The sacrament is a rite of initiation through which people become members of the Church. The word 'baptise' means to immerse in water. Water is used as a symbol of the washing away of sin.

Reason is the process of logical thought; the ability to think in a logical way, to form judgements and opinions through rational and evidence-based consideration.

Confirmation is a rite through which a person who has been baptised (particularly one baptised as an infant) affirms their Christian belief and is recognised as a full member of the Church.

Eucharist means 'thanksgiving' and is also called 'Holy Communion'. The service which celebrates the death and resurrection of Jesus. Bread and wine represent (or, as some Christians such as Catholics believe, actually become) the body and blood of Jesus. The Eucharist is a re-enactment of the Last Supper.

Pilgrimage is a journey made to a sacred place as an act of worship or devotion, e.g. Christians may visit Jerusalem to walk in Jesus' footsteps.

Free will is the ability to make choices (particularly moral choices) voluntarily and independently. The belief that nothing is predetermined.

Heaven is a place in the afterlife where those who have accepted God's grace and forgiveness in this life will enjoy an eternal existence in God's presence in the next life.

Hell is a place of punishment in the afterlife for those who, through their own free will, reject God's grace and forgiveness and will have chosen to live eternally outside of God's presence.

Vows are promises made between people or a person's promise to God. Wedding vows are promises the bride and groom make, committing themselves to one another.

Marriage symbols are features of the wedding ceremony that indicate the purpose and meaning of marriage. For instance, the wedding ring, being a continuous circle of precious metal, symbolises the never-ending, precious love between the bride and the groom.

Beliefs and practices

REVISED

Your study of Christianity's core beliefs, teachings and practices is separated into two areas:
- Beliefs:
  - The Bible
  - The afterlife
- Practices:
  - Life's journey
  - Special places

Differences matter

In your studies it is expected that you will learn about the different interpretations, attitudes and practices between some of the varied traditions of Christianity, such as Church in Wales, Catholic and Protestant churches, Evangelical traditions and the Society of Friends. The table below will help you remember why people who follow the same religion may hold different views.

Situation	Some situations, such as the importance of saving life, are important for all practising Christians, but for other situations there will be different considerations (e.g. the nature of heaven and hell).
Teachings	The central teachings considered by Christians would be the Bible. Some Christians regard it as the inspired Word of God, but most believe it was revealed by God as a source of authority to help people to live out their lives as Christians. The example and teaching of Jesus, as recorded in the Gospels and referred to in other New Testament, are another source of authority for Christians.
Authority	As well as the Bible, many Christians take into account other sources of authority, such as ministers or priests, teachings of the Church, the Holy Spirit and individual conscience.
Interpretation	Some Christians believe the Bible is literally true. Many others believe it is important to consider the teachings of the Bible for contemporary society.
Reason	Most Christians are in agreement that God gave people free will to choose to follow the example and sayings of Jesus. Regular reading of the Bible, prayer and worship are thought to help believers 'follow the way' (of Jesus) and make the right decisions and actions.

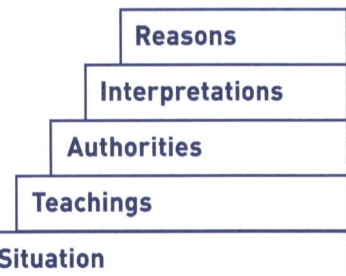

> **Exam tip**
>
> Since there are many different beliefs, teachings and practices in Christianity, it is important to show you understand this diversity. When answering questions, use phrases that indicate this range: 'some Evangelical Christians …', 'often many Catholic Christians …', 'some from the Society of Friends might …'

Beliefs: the Bible

In this area of study you will be expected to know beliefs and teachings about **the Bible**, its makeup, how it is used, the different ways in which it is interpreted and how it relates to other forms of authority for Christians.

> The Bible is a special and sacred book because it is believed to be the Word of God. It tells the story of God making himself known to people in their lives and situations, and so has ultimate authority.

> **Key concept**
>
> **The Bible** is the Christian sacred text believed by Christians to be revealed and/or inspired by God, made up of the Old and New Testaments.

The Bible as the Word of God

REVISED

What is the Bible?	• The Bible is the sacred text for Christians. • It is a collection of 66 separate books (although Catholics recognise 73 and Orthodox churches recognise 76). • It was written by 40 different people over thousands of years.
Why is it important?	• It is believed to have been a **revelation** from God in some way. • All Christians believe the Bible contains teachings that come from God. • Some believe the Bible contains metaphors and symbols, not literal truth, but it is still important.
Why is it called the 'Word of God'?	• Christians believe the Bible is not an ordinary book but the Word of God. • To some, this means it is literally true, dictated by God, as it were, to the different writers. • To others, it means that God influenced the writers as they worked.

> To reveal something is to make known what was previously hidden. To many Christians, the Bible makes known things about God that otherwise would not be known. It is inspired by God, helps believers understand more about God, and contains divine laws and clear guidance about how to live life according to God's ways.

> **Key concept**
>
> **Revelation** is God making himself known to humankind; for instance, through the Bible.

> **Activity**
>
> **The Bible as the Word of God: differing ideas**
>
> Look at the information on differing Christian views about the Bible and complete a Venn diagram like the example below.
>
> After creating your Venn diagram, use the information in it to explain why some Christians are literalists (they believe the Bible is literally true) and why some are non-literalists (they believe the Bible is symbolic or metaphorical).

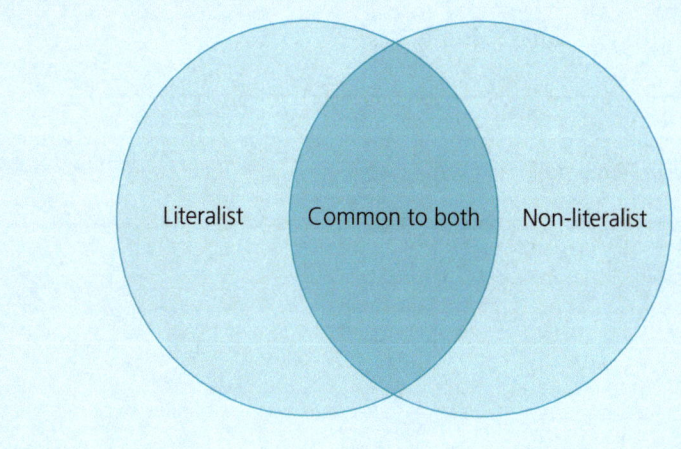

> **Exam tip**
>
> In any religious tradition there will be different interpretations. Your answers should show diversity of beliefs and practices.

Christianity: core beliefs, teachings and practices

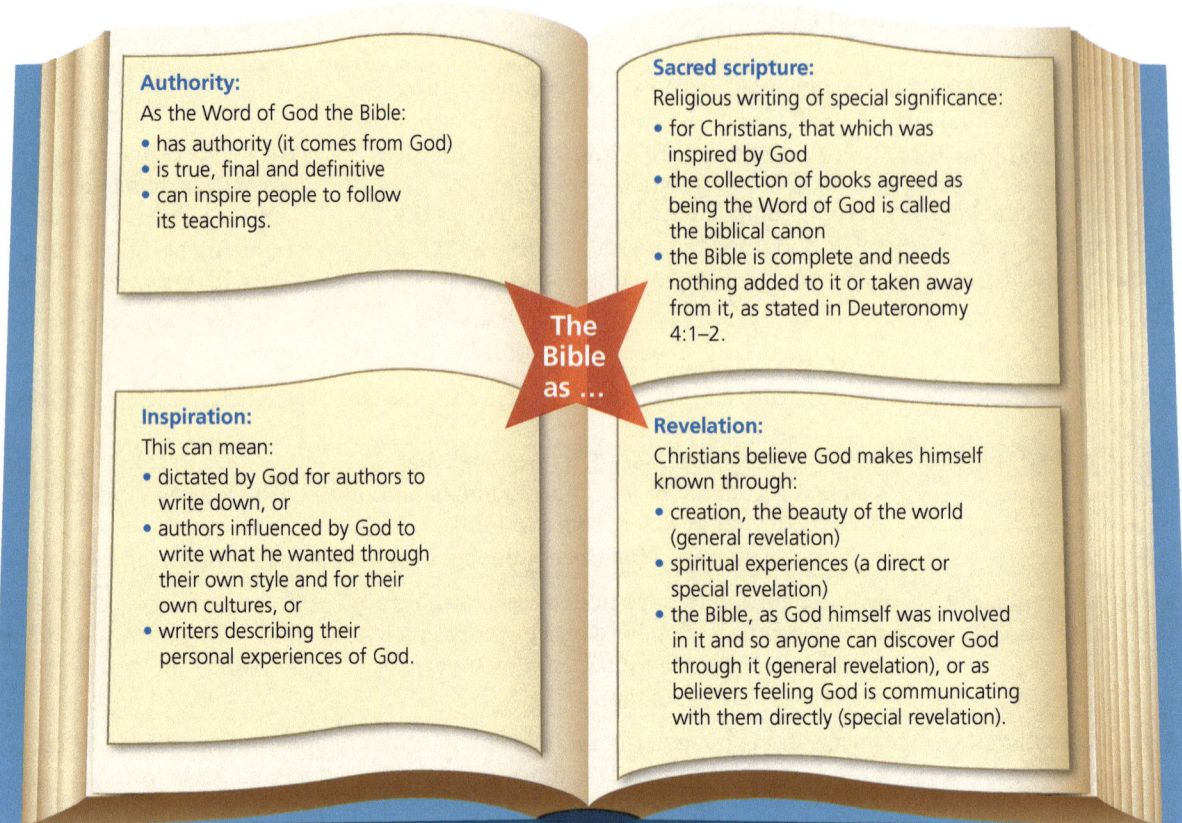

The Bible as a collection of writings

REVISED

The Bible is a collection of books. Each is different because of **A**uthorship, the author's **I**ntentions, the **A**udience, the **C**ontext and the **S**ociety in which it was written. The figure below will help you to remember these key points:

🔍 **Authorship** – who wrote it?
🔍 **Intentions** – why did the person write it?
🔍 **Audience** – for whom was it written?
🔍 **Context** – what else was taking place at the time of writing?
🔍 **Society** – in which culture was it written?

Aiming to understand the Bible with these questions in mind is known as historical criticism.

> **Activity**
>
> Using the information above, write your own paragraph that includes two different ways that Christians think of the Bible.

Uses and usefulness of the Bible

REVISED

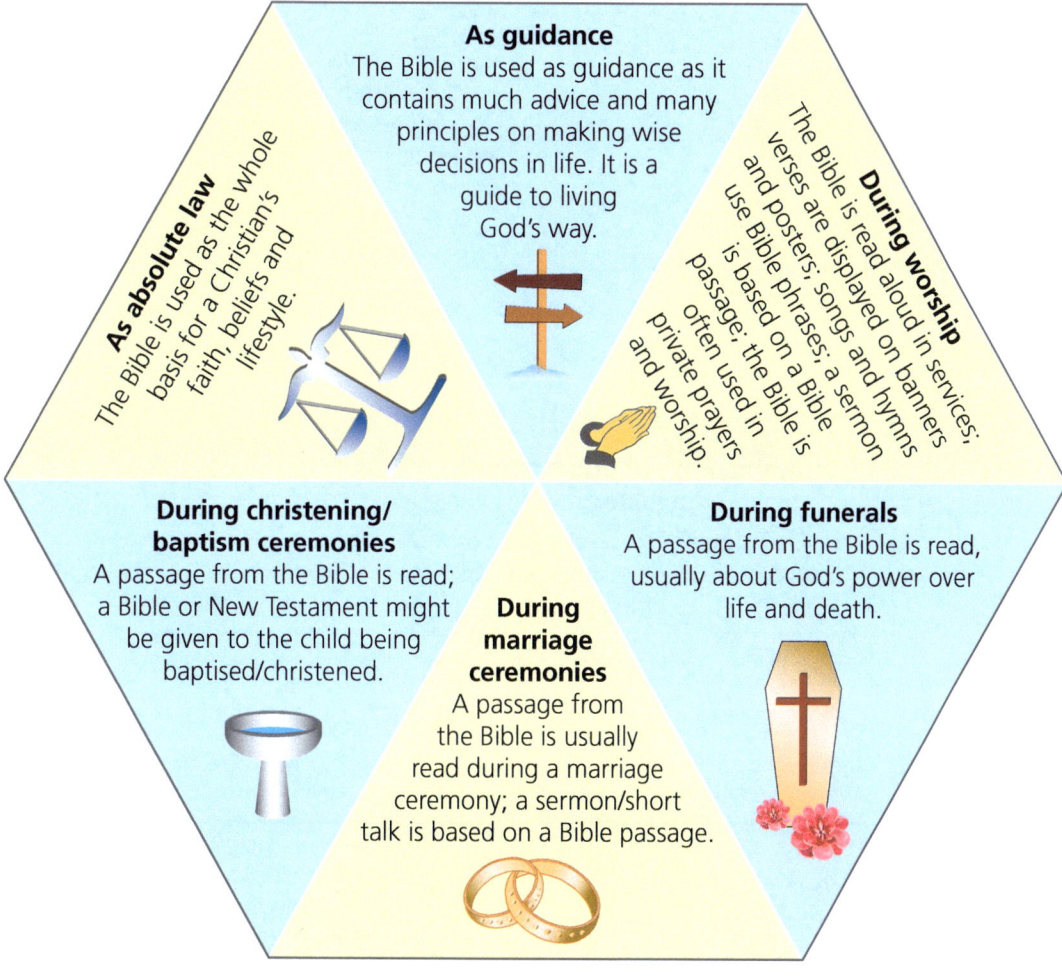

Many Christians refer to 2 Timothy 3:16–17, which states the Bible is useful for:
- 'teaching': about the Christian faith
- 'rebuking': providing guidance on ethics
- 'correcting': telling people how to change their outlook
- 'training in righteousness': learning how to live the 'right' way, as God requires
- equipping Christians to do all that God asks of them.

> **Exam tip**
>
> If you can refer to relevant sources of wisdom, or sacred texts, to support your answer it will help you get high marks. You don't need to remember the exact words or references, but state in your own words what they say and how believers interpret them.

> **Activity**
>
> Using the information above, construct your own 'Give me 5' (as on page 12, for example) memory aid on the use of the Bible.

Different ways of interpreting biblical writings

REVISED

Literal: the actual words of God; everything is accurate, nothing is false; they reject science where it conflicts with biblical views.

Conservative: true and without error, but written by humans inspired or influenced by God; they accept scientific views alongside biblical truths.

Different ways of interpreting the Bible.
All Christians describe the Bible as the Word of God, but they see it as such in four different ways:

Biblical myth: written by authors in pre-scientific days, who used cultural stories to express their understanding; literal interpretations are seen as too narrow and non-defendable in a scientific age.

Symbolic: stories and events have layers of meaning with spiritual significance.

> **Exam tip**
>
> **Understanding 2-mark A questions**
>
> In this unit there will be an A question that carries 2 marks. In order to gain 2 marks you need to either make two relevant points or make one point that you develop, explain or elaborate in some way.

> **Activity**
>
> Look at the three examples of answers to what Christians mean by 'revelation' below and decide how many marks you would give to each and why.
> - Example 1: Showing something clearly.
> - Example 2: God making himself known to human kind – for instance, through the Bible.
> - Example 3: God showing himself, as through Jesus.

The Bible in relation to other sources of authority

REVISED

Although Christians use the Bible, there are other sources of authority they may use. These include:

Society

This is a great influence on people and often Christian practices reflect the society in which they live; for example, some churches in India expect Christian worshippers to remove shoes when entering a church.

Reason

Many Christians believe God gave humans **reason** – the process of logical thought. Christians may use reason to decide on their use of wealth (Theme 2: Issues of wealth and poverty).

> **Key concept**
>
> **Reason** is the process of logical thought; the ability to think in a logical way, to form judgements and opinions through rational and evidence-based consideration.

Conscience

Many Christians believe that conscience is God-given so it is wise to follow it. St Paul in Romans 2:14–15 refers to people's 'consciences also bearing witness', which means that it is wise to listen to one's conscience. Christians may follow their conscience in issues of sex and relationships (Theme 1: Sexual relationships).

Circumstances

Some people believe that decisions should be made in an individual circumstance based on love and the best thing to do in that circumstance. Some Christians might argue against this because they believe that Bible teaching is absolute, for example relative and absolute morality (Theme 2: Crime and punishment).

Situations

Some Christians believe it is important to weigh up each situation and decide what is the most loving thing to do, based on the laws of the Bible and the teachings of Jesus, for example attitudes to abortion (Theme 1: Origin and value of human life).

Civil law

Civil laws within the United Kingdom are about relationships between people, or between people and institutions, for example conflict between personal religious conviction and the laws of a country (Theme 2: Human rights and social justice).

Family

Christians believe family life is where children can learn how to behave, for example Theme 1: Relationships.

> **Exam tip**
>
> **Making connections**
>
> The content in this section about beliefs in life after death and in judgement will have many links with the Philosophical Themes you have to study, in particular Issues of Human Rights.

> **Activity**
>
> *The Bible is all that Christians use to make judgements.*
>
> How might someone respond using three of the following?
> - Conscience
> - Family
> - Reason
> - Society
> - Situation
> - A civil law
> - Circumstances

Beliefs: the afterlife

In this area of study you will need to know about Christian beliefs in life after death, judgement, resurrection, and heaven and hell.

Belief in life after death

REVISED

- There is eternal life after death, received through faith. (John 3:16: 'whoever believes in him … shall have eternal life'; Matthew 25:46: '… the righteous [those who respond to Jesus and those in need in the world] go to eternal life.')
- Entry to heaven depends on a person's response to Jesus, their repentance, and to those in need on earth.
- Resurrection is expected, because of the resurrection of Jesus. (John 11:25: 'I am the resurrection and the life. The one who believes in me will live, even though they die.')
- There is a hell – the opposite of heaven – a place of separation from God. (Matthew 25:46: '… then they [who have not responded to Jesus or those in need in the world] will go away to eternal punishment …'
- Catholics believe there is a purgatory, a place of cleansing that is between earth and heaven; prayers can be said for those in purgatory, to shorten their stay there.

Belief in judgement, responsibility for action and free will

REVISED

- There will be a **judgement** day, when the quality of people's lives will be judged by God (like a shepherd separates sheep and goats, Matthew 25:31–46).
- This will be the time that Jesus comes for a second time – 'the Parousia'.
- It will be the end of human existence on the earth.
- There will be bodily resurrection of the dead, and believers will be transformed into a glorified state. (Luke 16:19–31 – the Parable of the Rich Man and Lazarus; 1 Corinthians 15:20–22 – in Christ all will be made alive.)
- A new heaven and a new earth will commence, with no tears, sorrow, sin or death.

There is a clear link, in Christian belief, between judgement, responsibility and **free will**. Because of free will, people can make decisions for themselves about their lifestyle and actions. Being able to do this brings the responsibility for the outcomes of the action or lifestyle, and if there is a judgement, as Christians believe, then there will be a reward or punishment in the light of decisions made.

> **Key concepts**
>
> **Judgement** is the belief that God will judge whether or not humans are worthy to enter the Kingdom of Heaven.
>
> **Free will** is the ability to make choices (particularly moral choices) voluntarily and independently. The belief that nothing is predetermined.

Answers at www.hoddereducation.co.uk/myrevisionnotesdownloads

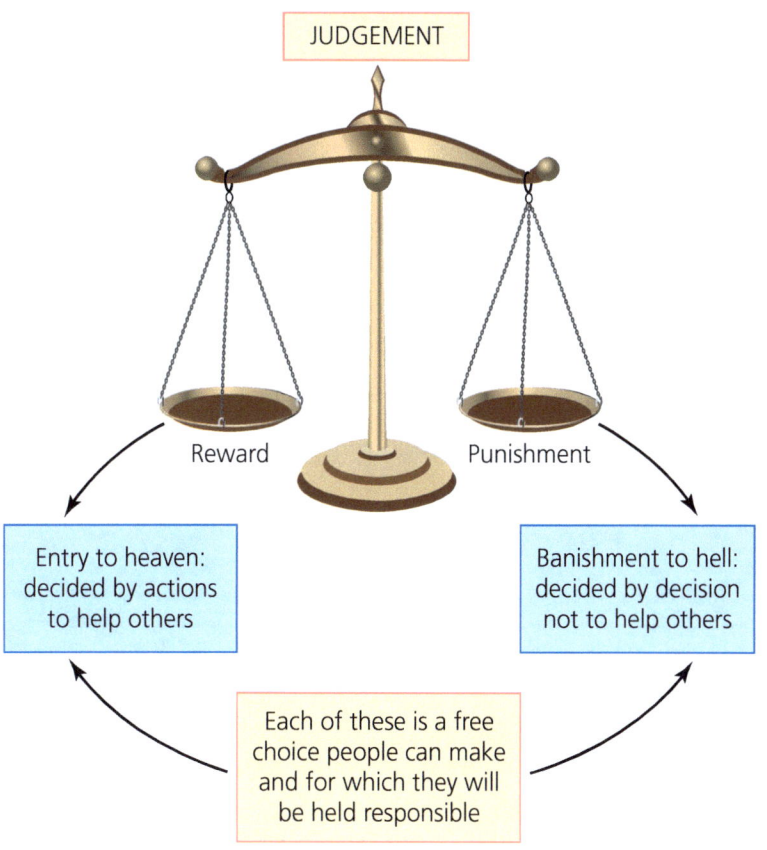

Exam tip

When you are asked to 'describe', make sure you select important points as you will have only about five minutes to write your answer.

Activity

Using some of the information in the table below, write three sentences that you could use to explain what the parable teaches in relation to free will, judgement and responsibility for actions.

The link between free will and judgement is shown in the Parable of the Sheep and the Goats (Matthew 25:31–46).

The 'sheep' – those rewarded by God		The 'goats' – those punished by God
What they did	The kinds of people they encountered	What they didn't do
Gave them food to eat	The hungry	No food given
Gave them a drink	The thirsty	No drink given
Invited them in	The stranger	No welcome given
Gave them clothes	Those needing clothes	No clothes given
Visited them in prison	Those in prison	No visiting while in prison

A key point to remember about judgement is that Christians believe people are not judged merely by good deeds but also by the faith they have, which motivates their actions.

Exam practice

8-mark C questions

'Explain Christian beliefs about Judgement Day.' [8 marks]

Look at the band descriptors for C questions on page 86. Using the information in the section above, write an answer that merits a Band 4 mark.

Make sure you include:
- detailed explanation of the beliefs
- awareness and insight into the beliefs
- use of religious/specialist language
- sources of wisdom/authority.

Answers online

Belief in resurrection

- The spiritual part of a person (soul) is able to be with God in heaven after death.
- Some Christians also believe that at the end of time there will be a physical resurrection – people will have new physical bodies, just as Jesus did after his resurrection.
- This final resurrection will also mark the 'Parousia', or 'second coming' of Jesus, when he will judge the living and the dead.
- St Paul frequently referred to the resurrection of the dead and specifically stated in 1 Corinthians 15:20–22 that just as sin and death came through Adam, so 'all in Christ will be made alive'.
- Because Christians believe Jesus was not just a human but God at the same time, they believe that all humans can overcome death through their faith in Jesus.

Belief in heaven and hell

There are many references to **heaven** and **hell** in the Bible, but there are different interpretations as to the actual meaning of the language of those passages where there is a description. However, Christians do have beliefs about heaven and hell and the main ones are summarised in the table on page 15.

> The question of what happens after life has fascinated all human societies. Christians believe in the holiness and justice of God, as well as his compassion and forgiveness. This means there is a time to give account for one's actions. Then there will be punishments and rewards. The belief in free will also impacts on beliefs in heaven and hell: the place to which a person goes is determined by their choice in terms of faith and action.

Key concepts

Heaven is a place in the afterlife where those who have accepted God's grace and forgiveness in this life will enjoy an eternal existence in God's presence in the next life.

Hell is a place of punishment in the afterlife for those who, through their own free will, reject God's grace and forgiveness and will have chosen to live eternally outside of God's presence.

Heaven

REVISED

What will heaven be like?	Most Christians believe heaven is the place to which believers go when they die; a place where God can be known clearly, and where earthly life and cares are forgotten. However, Christians also have differing views about heaven: some think it is an actual, physical place; others believe it is more of a spiritual dimension or existence. But for most Christians there is also the firm belief that there will be a new heaven and a new earth – a place where there is no more sorrow, sin or death. That is the heaven of eternal life and immortality - where God will be the centre and focus of all who live there, forever.
When will it happen?	Christians believe that those who have faith in Jesus go to heaven when they die. Catholics would say only very good believers go straight to heaven, and the rest go to purgatory first, to be cleansed and made ready for heaven.
Why is it important?	Many Christians would say that only those who have faith in Jesus and his death and resurrection will go to heaven. It is to be in the presence of God. Heaven will be a paradise – Jesus referred to this, as in Luke 16. Heaven is also seen as a reward for a life of faith and good works. Others would argue that as God is omnibenevolent all will ultimately be forgiven and enter into a new relationship with God in heaven.

Hell

REVISED

What will hell be like?	Most Christians believe it is a place of suffering, even torment. This is because, whatever else it might be, it is a place of absolute separation from God and all that comes from his presence and love. Christians also have differing views about hell: some think it is a physical place, where people burn eternally; other believe that if it exists, it is a kind of spiritual dimension, but one that does not include God.
When will it happen?	Christians believe it is the place to which people go when they die if they have rejected Jesus. Many Christians also believe that it is an eternal place; a place where, after judgement day, those without faith will remain - always separated from God and his goodness.
Why is it important?	Most Christians believe hell is to be absent from the presence of God. Jesus' teachings refer to it (as in Luke 16). Some Christians believe hell is a punishment for a life without atonement.

Activity

'The existence of hell does not fit with a belief in an all loving God.' Select two arguments from each hand and explain why each argument would be important to use in your answer.

On the one hand:
- Jesus referred to hell in his teachings.
- Jesus taught that people have a choice through their actions of going to heaven or hell.
- Hell is a state of being separated from God.

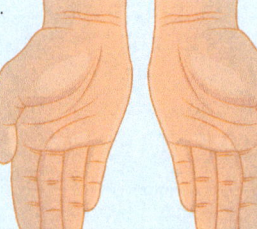

On the other hand:
- Jesus taught about the love of God.
- If God is omnibenevolent then how can hell exist?
- People can change their beliefs close to death.
- If God's love is shown through the sending of Jesus to Earth, then why would God want to make people suffer in hell?

	Point	Explanation
Left hand point 1		
Left hand point 2		
Right hand point 1		
Right hand point 2		

Practices: life's journey – sacraments and key acts of worship

In this area of study you will need to know about four sacraments/key acts of worship: baptism, Eucharist/Communion, confirmation, marriage. You should know the reasons and rituals involved for baptism, the differing interpretations and associated practices of Eucharist/Communion, the preparation and ceremony of confirmation, and the significance of a religious wedding and the symbols and vows associated with it.

Sacraments are an outward sign of an invisible and inward blessing by God, and mark the stages of a Christian's life journey. There are different views about which key acts of worship are sacraments in the various traditions within Christianity.

Baptism

REVISED

Baptism is a ceremony that welcomes a person into the community of Christians, the Church. The main aspects of baptism are shown in the table below.

> Christians believe that every person's sin can be cleansed away. Baptism is the ceremony that symbolises that 'cleansing'. Infant baptism is when the parents have chosen for their child. Believers' baptism is when a person old enough decides for themselves.

Key concept

Baptism The sacrament is a rite of initiation through which people become members of the Church. The word 'baptise' means to immerse in water. Water is used as a symbol of the washing away of sin.

What is baptism?	It is an initiation into the Christian church family. For some Christians (Anglican and Catholic) it is a sacrament and marks the entry of a child into the Christian family. Parents and God-parents make promises to bring them up in the Christian way of life. For others, it is a rite, and indicates a person's choosing to be a member of the Christian family, and showing obedience to the example of Jesus.
When does it happen?	For some Christians (Anglicans and Catholics), it is babies or young children who are baptised at a font. Sometimes this is called 'christening', and often takes place at the end of a service of worship, but can be arranged separately. For others, (Baptists and Pentecostals), it is usually a baptism by immersion, which takes place during a normal service of worship, and is for anyone old enough to decide for themselves that they want to follow the Christian way of life.
Why is baptism important?	Baptism is a rite of entry marking people's membership of the Christian Church. It is also believed by some to indicate the removing of sin. Jesus himself was baptised as an adult. For some traditions baptism is a public show of personal faith. Those practising 'believer's baptism' see the person being united with Christ, including in his death and resurrection. John 3:3–6 – refers to a spiritual birth: 'born of water and the Spirit'; this is essential to being 'born again' – not physically, but spiritually.

Eucharist/Communion

REVISED

The **Eucharist** or Communion service is a key act of Christian worship for all Christians.

Because Christians believe in Jesus as the Son of God and Saviour, the Eucharist or Communion service which commemorates his death is very significant. Jesus himself told his followers to share this service in memory of him, so Christians feel a special closeness to God: they find their faith is strengthened and renewed through celebrating this special 'meal'.

Key concept

Eucharist means 'thanksgiving' and is also called 'Holy Communion'. The service which celebrates the death and resurrection of Jesus. Bread and wine represent (or, as some Christians such as Catholics believe, actually become) the body and blood of Jesus. The Eucharist is a re-enactment of the Last Supper.

What is the Eucharist?	It is a service to remember the death of Jesus, and includes the bread and wine used by Jesus at the Last Supper with his disciples. Christians see the bread as a symbol of the body of Jesus, and the wine as a symbol of his blood. Some traditions, such as Anglican and Catholic, refer to it as a sacrament, and often call it Eucharist. Catholics refer to it as 'Mass'. Other traditions, such as Protestant churches see it as an important memorial service, and often call it 'Communion', 'Breaking Bread', or 'The Lord's Supper'.
When does it happen?	For Anglicans and Catholics, the Eucharist or Mass will usually take place every Sunday morning, and on other special occasions or services. Protestants tend to have it less frequently, often using a twice monthly pattern, as well as at special times like Easter or Christmas. It is either a part of the normal service of worship, or is added to the end of a service.
Why is the Eucharist important?	It was instituted by Jesus at the Last Supper, and the bread and wine are symbols of the body and blood of Jesus given so that people could receive salvation (1 Corinthians 11:23–26). Jesus told his followers to share the bread and wine in memory of his death for them. The word 'Eucharist' means 'thanksgiving', and is a thanksgiving for the life and death of Jesus and for the Christian faith. For Anglicans and Catholics, it is a liturgical service, and has a set pattern and structure that is followed each time. Others also have patterns and forms of the celebration, but it is not necessarily set out and followed strictly each time it is celebrated.

Confirmation

REVISED

The service of **confirmation** is a ceremony that enables a person to confirm that they are now making their personal choice to follow the Christian faith.

The purpose of the confirmation service is to allow baptised children to confirm it is their own desire to follow Christ and grow in their Christian faith and practice. The disciples were filled with the Holy Spirit at Pentecost (Acts 2:1–13) and Christians believe this can be passed on through the laying on of hands. The bishop will place his hands on candidates at a confirmation service.

Key concept

Confirmation is a rite through which a person who has been baptised (particularly one baptised as an infant) affirms their Christian belief and is recognised as a full member of the Church.

Preparation for confirmation

Someone who wants to be confirmed will usually attend confirmation classes, which will include prayer, Bible study, discussion and instruction. Classes are conducted by the priest or vicar of the church which the candidates for confirmation attend and may use a course guide published by the Church. The purpose is to ensure that candidates fully understand the commitment they are choosing to make.

The confirmation ceremony

Symbols of confirmation	Significance of the symbols
Laying on of hands (usually by the bishop who conducts the confirmation ceremony)	The calling down of the Holy Spirit to the person, to enable them to live their Christian life.
Anointing with oil	Chrism oil was used to anoint kings; it reflects that the candidate is being prepared for an important role.
Words of the Liturgy	The service confirms that the person is now a member of the Church.
Sign of peace	Use of the peace handshake or embrace indicates unity as members of the Christian Church.

Christian traditions have differences, as shown in the table below.

Catholic: • performed in the candidate's parish church • conducted by the bishop • bishop lays hands on candidate • bishop makes sign of the cross on their forehead with chrism oil • candidates often take on a saint's name • Holy Communion will follow (it will be the first Communion for the candidates).	Church in Wales: • conducted by the bishop • candidates renew the promises made for them at baptism • bishop lays hands on candidates' heads • prayers are said • sometimes water may be sprinkled on foreheads and/or anointing with chrism oil.
Methodist: • conducted by ministers • perform the laying on of hands, reciting a prayer.	Baptist: • confirmation is not performed as babies are not baptised, only those old enough to be aware of the commitment they are making.

Significance of a religious wedding: matrimonial symbols and vows

REVISED

Today it is possible to have a civil wedding or a religious one. For religious people, marriage is a relationship in which God himself is involved and so is a binding and lifelong relationship. Jesus says, in Mark 10:7–9, 'therefore what God has joined together, let no one separate'.

In most Christian wedding celebrations there are **marriage symbols** and **vows**. These indicate the solemn and serious nature of the commitments involved in a marriage.

> For Christians, marriage is an important relationship and ceremony in which God himself is involved, so symbols help to remind people of the important and significant aspects of what the commitment involves.

Key concept

Marriage symbols are features of the wedding ceremony that indicate the purpose and meaning of marriage. For instance, the wedding ring, being a continuous circle of precious metal, symbolises the never-ending, precious love between the bride and groom.

Because Christians believe that marriage is a God-ordained relationship and that it is a lifelong commitment, vows are said by the couple in the presence of God and witnesses, affirming that they understand the commitment and agree to it willingly.

> **Key concept**
>
> **Vows** are promises made between people or a person's promise to God. Wedding vows are promises the bride and groom make, committing themselves to one another.

Marriage symbols	The symbolism
Rings	The never-ending love of the couple for each other; a symbol of the lifelong commitment of marriage. (Often used but not essential in a wedding.)
Veil	The bride's purity in coming to the marriage; it is removed to symbolise the two individuals becoming one through the marriage.
Vows	The deep commitment the couple are making to each other – not just a promise, a lifelong commitment.
Crowns	The presence of God, and that a new family has been created, led by a king and a queen as it were. (In Orthodox marriages the priest places golden crowns on the heads of the bride and groom.)
Candles	Lit candles held during the ceremony by the bride and groom symbolise their willingness to receive the light of Christ (in Orthodox marriages).

Marriage vows	What they might mean
To have and to hold	The couple will support and care for each other in their new life together.
From this day forward	The wedding day marks a new beginning in the couple's relationship and life together, now as husband and wife.
For better for worse	The marriage will involve good and bad times, and the couple's commitment to each other is to last through both those kinds of experiences.
For richer for poorer	There will be times in marriage of wealth and good fortune, as well as times of financial testing and difficulty, and the commitment is to face these together.
In sickness and in health	There will be times in their life together when one or both are not in good health and their commitment is to support each other at those times.
To love and to cherish	Their new life together is one of loving and caring for each other, practically, emotionally and sexually.
Till death do us part	The marriage is expected to be a lifelong commitment; the only thing to end it should be the death of one of the couple.
According to God's holy law	The marriage is ordained by God and involves God as well as the couple; it is part of his plan for human beings.
And this is my solemn vow	The commitment is a serious one and is not to be revoked or broken.

> **Activity**
>
> Choose three of the vows listed below and write a suitable explanation, giving examples of what this would mean in a marriage:
> - To have and to hold
> - From this day forward
> - For better or worse
> - For richer for poorer
> - In sickness and in health
> - To love and to cherish
> - Till death do us part
> - According to God's holy law
> - And this is my solemn vow

Christianity: core beliefs, teachings and practices

Practices: special places

In this area of study you will need to know about the significance of a place of worship and the purpose and activities of different places of pilgrimage in Wales and elsewhere.

Significance of places of worship

- A place of worship is set aside for devotion and worship, usually consecrated. There are many different names; for example, church, chapel, cathedral, house church.
- In a place of worship people feel closer to God, as it separates daily living activities from worship times and rituals.
- Jesus himself confirmed the idea of people feeling closer when he said in Matthew 18:20: 'Where two or three are gathered together in my name, there I am with them.'
- The two Greek words translated as 'church' in the New Testament are *ecclesia* (called out) and *kuriakos* (belonging to the Lord). These terms indicate the special significance of places of worship: a place for those 'called out' to serve God and a place for those to meet who 'belong to the Lord'.
- Gathering in places of worship encourages believers to love and to do good deeds (Hebrews 10:24–25). They encourage and support each other in living out the life of faith in their local community.

Exam practice

15-mark D questions

'Where a person worships simply isn't important.' [15 marks]

Discuss this statement, showing that you have considered more than one point of view. (You must refer to religion and belief in your answer.)

Select four points from the numbered statements below that you think are most important and use them to form your answer. In your response you must make sure you have:
- selected alternative or different viewpoints
- shown how belief influences individuals, communities and societies
- formed judgements
- taken no longer than 15 minutes to write your response.

1. Jesus said, 'Where two or three are gathered in my name, I am with them.' That suggests you can worship anywhere.
2. The church is not a building, it's the people.
3. Jesus taught people how to pray, and not to just pray in special places.
4. A church or chapel is 'God's House', so worship could take place there.
5. Worship is aided by a place designed for it, e.g. to focus on God sometimes through images, statues, furniture, stained glass, etc.
6. A church gives access to communal worship, teaching/preaching, Communion, rites of passage.
7. Worshipping in a place of pilgrimage is a powerful experience.
8. The Bible says to not neglect meeting together – this is less likely to happen where there is a recognised place for worship.

Answers online

Purpose of pilgrimage, places, activities, experiences in Wales and elsewhere

REVISED

A **pilgrimage** is a journey to a sacred place and is an act of religious devotion.

Christians may choose to go on pilgrimage for many reasons, such as to strengthen faith, visit places connected with Jesus, experience healing, or as an act of penance or saying sorry. The examples below give further details.

Key concept

Pilgrimage is a journey made to a sacred place as an act of worship or devotion, e.g. Christians may visit Jerusalem to walk in Jesus' footsteps.

Christian pilgrimage

- A journey to a sacred place, usually as an act of religious devotion.
- The Holy Land, 'travelling in the footsteps of Jesus' has always been popular.
- Pilgrimage is faith in action: the journey representing a Christian's journey from earth to heaven.
- It is an experience that is likely to deepen or develop spiritual faith.
- Sometimes there is a specific reason for the pilgrimage, e.g. healing, rededication or thanksgiving.

The Holy Land

- The Holy Land is a favourite with pilgrims as it is the land where Jesus lived, so people can 'follow in his footsteps'.
- Nazareth is where Jesus was brought up and spent most of his life. It was also where his birth was announced, so pilgrims often visit the Church of the Annunciation.
- Bethlehem is where Jesus was born, so the Church of the Nativity is a place where pilgrims can feel a sense of closeness to God.
- Jerusalem is where Jesus spent the last weeks of his life, so pilgrims visit the Garden of Gethsemane and other sites connected with Jesus' crucifixion for prayer and reflection.
- All of these are special to Christians and help to strengthen their faith and bring a deeper understanding of God.

St David's

- At the cathedral in St David's (West Wales) a shrine contains St David's bones.
- St David is important as the patron saint of Wales.
- There is a pilgrimage centre at St David's (Ty'r Pererin, or Pilgrim's House), which offers worship, prayer, hospitality, healing sessions and time to reflect on the life of St David.
- Special days with a programme of activities are also available, which help pilgrims think about their own life pilgrimage.
- Pilgrimage to St David's helps some Christians strengthen and deepen personal faith.

Bardsey Island

- There was a Christian community on the island from the sixth century and there are remains of a thirteenth-century monastery: this encourages pilgrims as they consider the many years of Christianity in the place.
- The site was important in the Middle Ages, as pilgrimage to the island was considered equivalent to two journeys to Rome.

- Pilgrims are able to worship in the ruins of the old chapel, or to use the new chapel on the island.
- Special programme days are available for pilgrims to help them develop their faith, for example through spiritual discussions.
- Pilgrims are helped in their faith and their determination through such experiences, for example sharing with other pilgrims.

St Non's Well

- It is said the well sprang up where St David was born to his mother, Non, and it is believed to have healing properties, so people throw in coins to ask for healing or for good outcomes.
- The site, a few miles from St. David's, was important in the Middle Ages; now pilgrims visit the chapel to reflect and contemplate the many years of Christian tradition.
- Today pilgrims place a pebble from the beach in front of David's stone, as thanks for answered prayers or special events in their lives. Some decorate the statue of St Non with rosary beads, money or other offerings.
- The site also has a modern chapel and a retreat house, which offers workshops and therapy, especially in bereavement.
- Pilgrims often find that they have been helped and encouraged in their faith through the experience.

The Pilgrim's Way

- This North Wales Way starts at Holywell, the site of Basingwerk Abbey and St Winefride's Well, also a place of pilgrimage in its own right.
- Following the Way allows pilgrims to experience a special time alone.
- There is the opportunity for companionship and fellowship at rest places.
- Completing the Way gives pilgrims a sense of real achievement.
- It's an opportunity to be separate from the ordinary, everyday things of life and through the pilgrimage come closer to God.

> **Exam tip**
>
> **B-type questions**
>
> These questions will ask you to describe a belief, teaching, practice or feature within the religion to show your knowledge and understanding of the topic. There are 5 marks available.

Exam practice

B-type questions

Describe what might happen on a Christian pilgrimage. [5 marks]

Look at the band descriptions for Band 3 answers on page 85. Select three of the points below and develop them into an answer that will gain the full 5 marks.
- Pilgrims visit places associated with their faith.
- Sometimes they seek healing in places such as Lourdes.
- Some Christians want to walk in Jesus' footsteps.
- Some pilgrims want to make penance.
- Christians are encouraged in their faith through a pilgrimage.
- They join with fellow believers from all over the world and gain more of a sense of Christian community and *ecclesia*.

Answers online

ONLINE

Judaism: core beliefs, teachings and practices

The big picture

Below is a summary of the key questions for this study of Judaism:
- Why are the Tenakh and Talmud important and how are they used in worship?
- What are the Abrahamic and Mosaic Covenants?
- Why are the Covenants important today?
- Why are the Ten Commandments important?
- Why are there different practices in observing the Ten Commandments?
- How are the mezuzah and Magen David symbols of Jewish identity?
- What are the symbols and ceremony of Brit Milah?
- What happens at a Bar/Bat Mitzvah and why is the ceremony important?
- How and why are tallit, tefillin and kippah worn by many Jews?
- What is the significance, preparation and celebration of Yom Hashoah, Rosh Hashanah, Yom Kippur and Pesach?

Key concepts

Tenakh is the Jewish sacred text comprising three sections: Torah, Nevi'im and Ketuvim.

Talmud is a collection of Jewish law and tradition; Mishnah and Gemara collected together. Study of the Talmud is an important religious duty for Jewish men.

Covenant is a solemn and binding promise or agreement between two parties. Covenants were made between God and Noah, Abraham and Moses.

Brit Milah is the ceremony of circumcision – removal of the foreskin of the penis on the eighth day after birth. It is regarded as a sign of God's covenant with his chosen people. Translates as 'Covenant of the Cutting'.

Bar Mitzvah means Son of the Commandment. A boy who reaches adulthood (age thirteen). It is usually marked by a synagogue ceremony and family celebration.

Bat Mitzvah means Daughter of the Commandment. A girl who reaches adulthood (age twelve). It is usually marked by a synagogue service and celebration.

Mezuzah literally means 'door post'. It is a scroll enclosed in a case (often decorative) placed on the right-hand door post of every room in a Jewish home.

Pesach is also called Passover or the Feast of Unleavened Bread. Festival commemorating the Exodus from Egypt, celebrated in the spring.

Magen David, the 'Shield of David', popularly called the Star of David. A six-pointed star which has become the symbol of Judaism. Its exact origin is unknown.

Abraham was the first Jew; the founder of Judaism. Abraham is believed to be the biological and spiritual ancestor of the Jewish people.

Moses was an important prophet. Moses led the Hebrews out of slavery in Egypt and took them to the Holy Land promised to them by God. He gave the Hebrews the Ten Commandments from God and is considered to be the only human to have encountered God directly (in the Burning Bush).

Promised Land, or the land of Canaan, was promised to Abraham and his descendants by God. Today it is known as Israel.

Tefillin are small leather boxes containing passages from the Torah, strapped on the forehead and arm for weekday, morning prayers. This is observed by Orthodox Jewish men of Bar Mitzvah age and over.

Beliefs and practices

REVISED

Your study of Judaism is separated into two areas:
- Beliefs:
  - Sacred texts
  - The Covenant
- Practices:
  - The use of sacred texts
  - Jewish identity

Differences matter

In your exam you will be expected to refer to the different attitudes and practices of Orthodox and Reform Jews. There are many views, but the table below will help you remember why so many different views are held by people who follow the same religion.

Situation	Some circumstances, such as idolatry and saving a life, are important for all practising Jews, but for other situations there will be different considerations, e.g. whether to wear a kippah.
Teachings	The central teachings referred to by Jews would be the Torah. The written Torah comprises the first five books of Moses: Genesis, Exodus, Leviticus, Numbers and Deuteronomy. Believed to have been given by God to Moses, many Jews will consult the Torah as a source of authority. One of the main differences between Orthodox and Reform Jews is that Orthodox Jews will observe the teachings of the written and oral Torah. Reform Jews will consider how they are compatible with a modern lifestyle.
Authority	There are many other sources of authority which Jews may consult in addition to the Torah, such as the Talmud, the teachings of historic rabbis such as Hillel and Maimonides, or the rabbi from a local synagogue.
Interpretation	Many Orthodox Jews will observe the Torah literally, with little or no interpretation. Many Reform Jews believe the teachings from the Torah and other sources of authority should be considered in the context of contemporary society and not always taken literally.
Reason	As Jews believe God gave them free will, so they believe it is up to them whether they follow a right inclination (Yetzer ha tov) or a bad inclination (Yetzer ha ra). Studying the Torah is believed to help them make a right decision.

Reasons
Interpretations
Authorities
Teachings
Situation

> **Exam tip**
>
> There are many different beliefs, practices and teachings in Judaism. Sometimes these depend on how observant a person is, the country they originated from or the influence of their family and friends. When answering questions, it is important to show this diversity, e.g. 'some Orthodox Jews might …' and 'often, many Reform Jews will….'.

> **Exam tip**
>
> **Making connections**
>
> Although the chapter is divided into the two sections of Beliefs and Practices, there are many connections. It is because of a particular belief that Jews will observe particular practices and celebrations. For example, because the Tenakh and Talmud are believed to be important, they are used in Jewish worship, prayer and study. There are also many connections with issues you are studying in the relationships, life and death, good and evil and human rights units. Relevant beliefs, texts and practices can be credited wherever they appear in your answers.

Beliefs: sacred texts

In this area of study you will be expected to know about the importance of the **Tenakh** as the revealed or inspired Word of God and the importance of the Talmud.

Importance of the Tenakh

REVISED

The three parts of the Tenakh are central to Jewish belief and worship and a guide for personal, family and community life. The Tenakh contains revelations and messages believed to come directly from God and writings inspired by God. It shows God's relationship from the beginning of creation to the life of Jews in the Promised Land.

> **Key concept**
>
> **Tenakh** is the Jewish sacred text comprising three sections: Torah (law), Nevi'im (the Prophets) and Ketuvim (Writings).

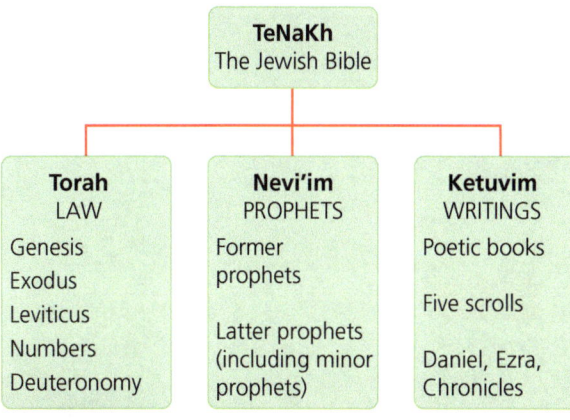

> **Exam tip**
>
> In the exam you may be asked questions about the importance of the Tenakh or about the importance of each of the three parts of the Tenakh (Torah, Nevi'im or Ketuvim). You must know the different contents of each and the different ways each is important to Jewish belief and practice.

	What does it contain?	Why is it important?
Torah	The books of Genesis, Exodus, Leviticus, Numbers and Deuteronomy. It includes the 613 mitzvot which Jews should follow (including the Ten Commandments).	Torah means law and contains the duties that Jews should observe. Many Jews believe that the Torah is the direct Word of God. It contains the history of the Jewish people from the creation until reaching the Promised Land.
Nevi'im	The work and teachings of prophets such as Joshua, Isaiah, Jonah and Amos.	Many Jews believe that the Nevi'im was not written by God but that God's messages were passed on through the teachings of the prophets. It contains many teachings about the importance of seeking justice and observing the duties set out by God in the Torah. It contains a history of the Jewish people after reaching the Promised Land.
Ketuvim	A collection of poetry, philosophy and history; writings such as the Psalms, which are sung in praise of God.	It was written by humans but many believe it is inspired by God. It contains stories from the division of the kingdom to the first return from exile.

> **Exam tip**
>
> It is important to use terms from the religions you have studied in your answers to examination questions. You will need to be able to define the concepts in each theme. The first exam question, for 2 marks, asks for a definition of a concept. To gain 2 marks you need to be able to give two separate points or a developed point.

Exam practice

A-type questions

What is meant by Tenakh? [2 marks]

Which of the answers below would you give 2 marks to? Give your reasons.
(a) The Tenakh is a Jewish holy book.
(b) The main part of the Tenakh is the Torah, which is the first five books and explains about the creation of the world and how Moses was called by God.
(c) The Tenakh is the main Jewish scripture, which is made up of three parts. These are the Torah (Law), the Nevi'im (Prophets) and the Ketuvim (Writings).

Answers online

ONLINE

Importance of the Talmud

REVISED

The **Talmud** is an important source of authority for Jews and has been passed down between generations of rabbis and students before being written down.

> **Key concept**
>
> **Talmud** is a collection of Jewish law and tradition; Mishnah and Gemara collected together. Study of the Talmud is an important religious duty for Jewish men.

What is the Talmud?	It is considered to be the Oral Torah. It was passed down through rabbis. There are two Talmuds (Babylonian and Jerusalem), but most Jews follow the Babylonian, which has more detailed discussions. It contains systems of laws based on the teachings of the Torah, with explanations of how they should be practised in daily life. It was passed down between generations of rabbis and students before being written down.
Why is it important?	Some Jews believe it was given by God to Moses at the same time as the written Torah and is therefore sacred. As it was passed down from rabbi to rabbi, it contains generations of wisdom. It gives interpretation of the Torah and includes case studies on how to observe the 613 mitzvot.
When is it used?	Many Jews study the Talmud as it is believed to be a sacred text and gives an understanding of Jewish belief and practice. The case studies are used to help make decisions on how the 613 mitzvot should be observed today.

Beliefs: the Covenant

In this area of study you will need to know about the meaning and significance of the Covenants made with Abraham and Moses and the importance of the Ten Commandments.

In Judaism, the relationship with God is seen as a covenant; it is like a contract when promises are made between two parties. Often the making of a covenant includes a special symbol, e.g. circumcision of male babies as a sign of the covenant with Abraham.

> **Key concept**
>
> **Covenant** is a solemn and binding promise or agreement between two parties. Covenants were made between God and Noah, Abraham and Moses.

Abrahamic Covenant

REVISED

Originally named Abram, God changed his name to Abraham, meaning 'father of many nations'. He was the first person to teach that there was only one God (monotheism).

The Land of Israel holds a special place in Judaism and is often called the Promised Land. The Tenakh teaches that it is chosen by God as holy. Many of the 613 mitzvot are connected with the Land of Israel and it is considered a mitzvah to live in Israel. For many Jews, certain places are particularly important:
- the Western Wall (the only remaining wall standing from the second Temple in Jerusalem)
- graves of great rabbis and scholars such as Maimonides.

In the Book of Genesis the three main parts of the **Covenant** made between God and **Abraham** are described:
- God called Abraham and his family to a new land called Canaan (Genesis 12:1–3). Abraham obeyed this command because he believed there was only one God and it was his duty to obey him. This land is now referred to as Israel and is often called the **Promised Land** because of God's repeated promise to give the land to the descendants of Abraham. Jews have lived there for more than 3,200 years. The Promised Land is identified with the Land of Israel and many Jews consider it their homeland given by God. Today many Jews from Wales choose to go on pilgrimages to Israel and visit holy sites.
- God promised Abraham he would make a great nation from him (Genesis 17:6–8). Abraham is considered as the founder of Jewish people and is often called 'father'.
- God promised to bless Abraham and his family. As a part of the Covenant, God gave Abraham the rite of circumcision (Genesis 17:11–14). Jewish male children are usually circumcised on the eighth day after birth to reflect their relationship with God (Brit Milah).

> **Key concepts**
>
> **Abraham** was the first Jew; the founder of Judaism. Abraham is believed to be the biological and spiritual ancestor of the Jewish people.
>
> **Promised Land**, or the land of Canaan, was promised to Abraham and his descendants by God (today known as Israel).

Activity

Identify how the parts of the Abrahamic Covenant show key beliefs and practices in Judaism today. Remember, a part of the Covenant may be used for more than one belief and practice.

Jewish identity	
Circumcision	
Belief in one god (monotheism)	
The Promised Land	

Mosaic Covenant

REVISED

Jews regard **Moses** as the greatest of the prophets. He is the only one to have spoken 'face to face' with God (Deuteronomy 34:10).

✋ Moses

- Moses had a special relationship with God and is considered the greatest prophet.
- Moses was chosen by God to lead the Israelites out of slavery in Egypt, but Moses thought he was not capable. However, God promised to be with him (Exodus 3:11–15).
- Moses is believed to be the only person who has seen God face to face.
- Moses was given the Torah by God on Mount Sinai and it is often called the Law of Moses. Orthodox Jews believe he was also given the Oral Torah, which is the commentary which discusses the Written Torah.
- Moses established a Covenant with God. As God's chosen people the Israelites would keep the commandments.

Key concept

Moses was an important prophet. Moses led the Hebrews out of slavery in Egypt and took them to the Holy Land promised to them by God. He gave the Hebrews the Ten Commandments from God and is considered to be the only human to have encountered God directly (in the Burning Bush).

> For me, like many Jews, reading the Torah (law) is important. It was given by God to Moses and the laws within it are for all time. Breaking any of these laws goes against my relationship with God.

> In the Torah are the commandments or mitzvot that God wants Jews to keep. These guide me on how I should live my life and treat other people. Some of my friends observe the duties literally while others adapt them for their lives today.

> God led Moses to the Promised Land and so I consider it important to visit and support Israel.

Activity

From the quotes above, identify how the Mosaic Covenant shows key beliefs and practices in Judaism today. Remember, a part of the Covenant may be used for more than one belief and practice.

Law (the Torah)	
Commandments	
Identity	
Promised Land	

Judaism: core beliefs, teachings and practices

Covenant today

REVISED

In this unit on Judaism you will find many examples showing how the Covenants made with Abraham and Moses impact on Jewish belief and practice today.

> **Activity**
>
> Finish the statements below by explaining the connection between the Covenant and Jewish practice today. Page numbers are given to support your explanations.
> - God promised to Abraham the Land of Israel. This is important for many Jews today because .... (page 27 about the Promised Land).
> - God gave Abraham the rite of circumcision. This is important today because .... (page 35 about Brit Milah).
> - Moses was chosen by God to lead the Israelites out of slavery. This is celebrated each year .... (page 41 about Pesach).
> - The importance of the Written Torah given by God to Moses is shown by .... (page 25 about the use of the Torah).
> - A part of the Torah given to Moses by God is the Ten Commandments. These .... (page 32 about the Ten Commandments today).

> **Activity**
>
> **Use of command terms**
>
> In the exam paper you will be asked four questions from this unit. Each of the questions will have different demands. In the table below, the meaning column has become jumbled. From the command word, try to identify which would be the correct meaning.
>
> | Command | Meaning |
> | --- | --- |
> | What is meant by ... [2 marks] | Evaluation of a view from more than one perspective. These perspectives can all be 'for' the statement, all be 'against' the statement or be a mixture of both 'for' and 'against', e.g. 'The Magen David is the best way to show Jewish identity.' Discuss this statement, showing that you have considered more than one point of view. (You must refer to religion and belief in your answer.) |
> | Describe ... [5 marks] | Definition of a key term (linked to one of the key terms identified for each unit), e.g. What is meant by Tenakh? |
> | Explain ... [8 marks] | Demonstrate knowledge and understanding by describing a belief, teaching, practice, event, etc., e.g. Describe how the Nevi'im is used. |
> | Discuss this statement, showing that you have considered more than one point of view. (You must refer to religion and belief in your answer.) [15 marks] | Demonstrate knowledge and understanding of a topic by explaining the statements made with reasoning and/or evidence, e.g.:
● Explain how ...
● Explain why ...
● Explain the main features of ...
● Explain the importance/significance of ...

For example: 'Explain the commemorations associated with Yom Hashoah.' |

Practices: the use of sacred texts

In this area of study you will need to know about the use of sacred texts.

In the last unit you learnt about the importance of the Tenakh and the Talmud. This unit builds on that knowledge and considers the different ways that the Tenakh and the Talmud are used. It is important to remember that, within the same religion, believers will interpret and practise the teachings from sacred texts in different ways and use them in daily life in different ways also.

The Tenakh and its use

REVISED

Tenakh: the Jewish sacred text comprising three sections: Torah, Nevi'im and Ketuvim

Worship
- Shabbat services begin with readings from the Book of Psalms (part of the Ketuvim).
- Portions (parashot) from the Torah are read each week in the Shabbat service.
- After the Torah reading a passage from the Nevi'im (prophets) is read.

Celebrations
- Jews will use the Tenakh to learn about the origins of festivals, e.g. Pesach.
- Reading from the Torah is a central feature for the Bar Mitzvah ceremony.
- Many celebrations have their origins in the Torah, e.g. the Brit Milah ceremony of circumcision is a symbol of the Covenant between God and Abraham, as described in the Torah (see page 27).

Prayer and study
- The Torah instructs Jews how to pray.
- Passages from the Torah and the Nevi'im are used for personal prayer.
- The Shema (see page 34) comes from the Torah and is central to morning and evening prayers.
- Studying the Torah is an important mitzvah. Synagogues have a house of study (bet midrash).
- Discussing and interpreting the Tenakh is important.
- The Nevi'im is read to learn more about the history of the Israelites.
- The Tenakh teaches Jews how they should behave through the mitzvot and the actions of the prophets.

✋ The Talmud as an explanation of the laws found in the Torah

REVISED

- It explains and interprets the laws in the Torah.
- It helps Jews understand their relationship with God.
- For Orthodox Jews it is as much the Word of God as the written Torah and so is a way to get closer to God.
- It is studied to advise Jews how they should react to contemporary situations, e.g. can fidget spinners be used on Shabbat?
- It is an important study for anyone wanting to be a rabbi.

> **Exam tip**
>
> **Use of sacred texts**
>
> If you can refer to relevant sources of wisdom or sacred texts to support your answer, it will help you get high marks. You don't need to remember the exact words or references, but you should state in your own words what they say and how believers interpret them. There are some texts in the Torah, such as the Ten Commandments, which are important for many areas of your study.

Exam practice

B-type questions

Describe how the Nev'im is used. [5 marks]

You have already learnt about the importance of the Tenakh and the Talmud. In your exam you might be asked to describe **what they are** or **how they are used** or both. Look at the answer below and decide what mark you would give and why. (Remember to use the mark bands on page 85.)

Answer 1: The Nev'im is part of the Tenakh and is therefore considered a sacred text by many Jews. It is read to learn more about the history of the Israelites from the death of Moses. It teaches about faith and justice and about the Covenant relationship between God and Israel. Passages from the Nev'im are often read in synagogues at the end of Torah readings.

Answer 2: The Tenakh is made up of three parts. The Torah, the Nevi'im and another. The Torah is the most important as the Torah scrolls are read from in the synagogue and many Jews believe it is the Word of God. The Nevi'im is important because it is read to learn the stories of the prophets such as Amos and how he tried to get justice.

Answers online

ONLINE

✋ Importance of the Ten Commandments

REVISED

- The Ten Commandments were given by God to Moses.
- They should be followed by all Jews.
- They are the duties required of humans for their creator God.
- They are the duties required for relationships between humans.
- They form the beliefs and practices of Judaism.

The Ten Commandments (Exodus 20:2–14) are an important part of your study. You will not be asked to write them all out but you should know what each of them says and how they relate to other parts of your study.

Their importance of the Ten Commandments can be seen in other areas of Judaism and the Philosophy and Ethics Issues. The table below shows these connections.

> **Exam tip**
>
> **Use of sacred texts**
>
> If you can refer to relevant sources of wisdom, or sacred texts to support your answer it will help you get high marks. You don't need to remember the exact words or references, but state in your own words what they say and how believers interpret them.

Making connections

Commandments	Connections
I am God Your Lord who has brought you out of Egypt from the place of slavery.	Celebration of Passover
Do not have any other gods before me.	Importance of the Shema Prayer No statues in synagogues.
Do not take the name of God in vain.	Censorship
Remember the Sabbath to keep it holy.	Preparing and celebrating Shabbat
Honour your father and mother.	The nature of the family
Do not commit murder.	Importance of *pikuach nefesh* (saving of life) Jewish attitudes to crime Jewish attitudes to abortion and euthanasia Jewish attitudes to the death penalty
Do not commit adultery.	Jewish attitudes towards adultery and relationships
Do not steal.	Jewish attitudes to crime
Do not testify as a false witness against your neighbour.	Jewish attitudes to justice Jewish attitudes to crime
Do not be envious of your neighbour's wife, his slave, his maid, his ox, his donkey, or anything else that is your neighbour's.	Jewish attitudes to crime Jewish attitudes to wealth

> **Exam tip**
>
> In your answers you can gain marks by making connections and applying relevant knowledge and text references from different areas of study. That means that what you have learnt in Judaism can be applied to questions in philosophy and ethics. The Ten Commandments is an example of this.

Diversity of practice within Judaism regarding observance of the Ten Commandments

REVISED

There are often different interpretations of sacred texts between Reform and Orthodox Jews. These interpretations impact how different people will observe the Ten Commandments in their daily practices and lifestyle. There are many ways that Jews worship in the home. Differences occur not only between Orthodox and Reform traditions but also within Orthodox and Reform families.

Although celebrated weekly, Shabbat is important for worship in both the home and the synagogue. There are many differences in the ways in which Orthodox and Reform Jews might celebrate Shabbat, but it is generally considered a time to focus on the important things of life.

Why is Shabbat important?	Keeping Shabbat obeys the mitzvah 'to remember' and to 'keep it holy' (Exodus 20:8). It is remembered as a celebration of God's creation. It is 'kept' through worship in the home and the synagogue.
	It is often seen as a gift from God, when weekday worries can be forgotten and families can be together. As the woman of the family lights the candles, so it is believed the presence of Shabbat bringing peace is brought into the home.
Why are there differences in practice?	Each family celebrates Shabbat in its own way.
	Most Orthodox Jews obey the teachings from the Torah and the Talmud and do not do any work during Shabbat.
	Many Reform Jews will try to set the day aside for spiritual and physical rest but will work if it is unavoidable.
What differences might there be?	It is important to remember that each family is different, but generally: • For Orthodox Jews, 'no work' means that driving and cooking are not allowed; nor is the carrying of anything, including money. Often Orthodox Jews will live near a synagogue, allowing them to walk to services. • Reform Jewish families will often interpret what is meant by 'no work'. For many this will allow them to drive to synagogue and to cook. However, most Reform Jews would celebrate Shabbat through family activities and acts of worship.

Practices: Jewish identity

In this area of study you will need to know about the many different ways that Jews might show their identity, including important symbols, ceremonies, what is worn and festivals.

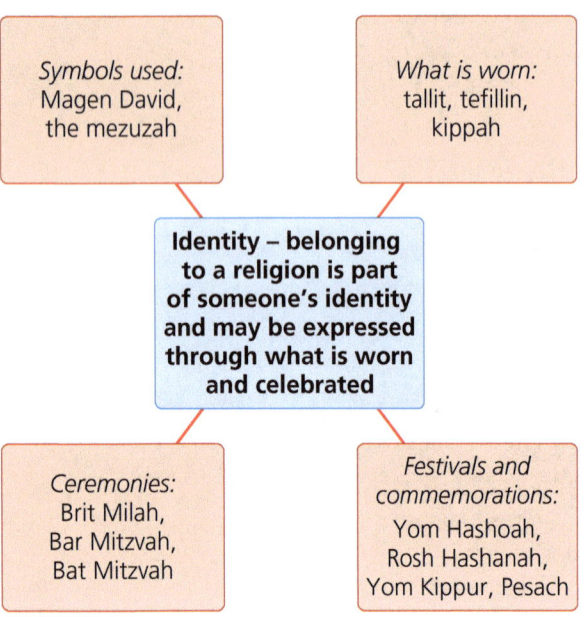

Symbols: the mezuzah and Magen David

REVISED

 ### Mezuzah

The **mezuzah** case is fixed to a door frame of every room except the bathroom or toilet.

- The Shema prayer is written on the mezuzah scroll. This is the most important prayer for Jews stating there is only one God.
- On the back of the scroll the word 'Shaddai' is written. This is one of the names for God.
- Jews will often touch the case as they pass through the door.
- After touching it they will kiss their fingers as a reminder of the Shema.
- For many Jews the mezuzah symbolises God's protection.

Key concept

Mezuzah literally 'door post'; a scroll enclosed in a case (often decorative) placed on the right-hand door posts of every room in a Jewish home.

Magen David

Although the **Magen David** might have little religious significance, many Jews wear or use it as a symbol of Jewish identity.

- There is no mention of the Magen David in the Torah or the Talmud.
- It is often considered a symbol for Jews and can be found on the Israeli flag and on many synagogues.
- Some believe it became a symbol of Jewish identity because soldiers of King David's army used shields in the shape of a six-pointed star.
- Some believe it became a symbol because the number six represents the heavens and earth plus the four directions (north, south, east and west), so showing God's omnipresence.
- In the lead-up to and during the Second World War, in Nazi-occupied lands Jews were forced to wear armbands bearing the Magen David.

> **Key concept**
>
> **Magen David**, 'Shield of David', popularly called the Star of David. A six-pointed star which has become the symbol of Judaism. Its exact origin is unknown.

Brit Milah

REVISED

For many Jewish parents the **Brit Milah** is important as it represents the relationship with God as in the Abrahamic Covenant, and also it is a symbol of Jewish identity.

What happens during the Brit Milah ceremony?	A mohel (mohelet) will circumcise the baby on the eighth day after birth. Usually only men attend the ceremony, although there will be women as well in Reform ceremonies. The baby is placed on an empty chair (Elijah's chair). Then the baby is placed on the lap of the sandek, who is chosen by the parents. After the circumcision the father says a blessing.
Why is a Brit Milah significant (important)?	It shows a relationship with God as it represents the Covenant made with Abraham. It does not make the baby a Jew but is a symbol that the baby or convert has entered into the Covenant.
What are the main symbols?	The circumcision represents the relationship with God as shown in the Abrahamic Covenant.
	Eight days is the number of days mentioned in the Torah (Leviticus 12:3). This ensures the baby will have experienced at least one Shabbat.
	Elijah's chair represents a belief that the Prophet Elijah visits every circumcision.
	Wine is shared by all (including a drop for the baby) to show this is a happy and sweet occasion.
	The baby is given a Hebrew name, which will be used at Bar Mitzvah and formal occasions in the synagogue.

> **Key concept**
>
> **Brit Milah** is the ceremony of circumcision – removal of the foreskin of the penis on the eighth day after birth. It is regarded as a sign of God's covenant with his chosen people. Translates as 'Covenant of the Cutting'.

Bar Mitzvah

REVISED

Usually Jewish boys prepare for their **Bar Mitzvah** well in advance of the day. It is a special occasion, marking a big step forward in their lives. That is why there is a family celebration afterwards.

Key concept

Bar Mitzvah means Son of the Commandment. A boy who reaches adulthood (age thirteen). It is usually marked by a synagogue ceremony and family celebration.

What happens during the ceremony?	Usually Jewish boys have a Bar Mitzvah ceremony on the Shabbat after their thirteenth birthday. Before a Bar Mitzvah the boy is taught about the importance of prayer and learns Hebrew so he can read his portion from the Torah in the synagogue. The boy is called up to the bimah in the synagogue to recite a blessing and read his part of the Torah. Friends and relatives watch. His father then recites a statement in which he thanks God. This is usually followed by a form of celebration.
Why is a Bar Mitzvah significant (important)?	It is a sign of entering into manhood and building a relationship with God. After a Bar Mitzvah boys can form part of the minyan (group of ten people needed for some prayers). They are believed to be responsible enough to keep the mitzvot in the Torah. Some Jewish boys will start to wear tefillin for prayers.
What are the main symbols?	The thirteenth birthday is the age of adulthood when a boy can enter into a covenantal relationship with God.
	From the Bar Mitzvah a boy can start to wear tefillin, which is a reminder that the wearer must serve God through developing good thoughts and through acts of compassion.
	The tallit is usually worn by the boy during the service.
	Wearing the tzizit relates to the duty to wear fringes in the corner of clothes (Numbers 15 in the Torah).

Bat Mitzvah

REVISED

Traditionally girls did not have a ceremony, but **Bat Mitzvahs** are becoming increasingly common.

Key concept

Bat Mitzvah means Daughter of the Commandment. A girl who reaches adulthood (age twelve). It is usually marked by a synagogue service and family celebration.

What happens in a Bat Mitzvah?	There are many different types of celebrations, which often depend upon the traditions of the family. Usually Bat Mitzvahs will include a special service in the synagogue and a presentation of the girl's learning. Reform Jews might read from the Torah scrolls during the service.
Why is Bat Mitzvah significant (important)?	Usually girls' ceremonies are not as large as a Bar Mitzvah as they are not required to do the same duties as boys. In Reform Judaism, after the Bat Mitzvah girls may be part of the minyan and read from the Torah scrolls.
What are the main symbols	The ceremony signals that the girl is taking on extra responsibilities.
	Some girls choose to wear a tallit as a reminder of Numbers 15 in the Torah.
	Sometimes a Kiddush cup is given, which will be used in the blessing of wine at Shabbat and is a reminder of the responsibilities the girl has as an adult.

Items worn for worship

REVISED

Many Jews choose to wear ritual items for worship. What they wear and when depends upon their interpretation of the Torah and the Talmud, how observant they are and their gender.

Tefillin

Learning how to wear the **tefillin** during worship is an important part of preparation for a boy's Bar Mitzvah. In some Jewish communities some females also wear tefillin.

> **Key concept**
>
> **Tefillin** are small leather boxes containing passages from the Torah, strapped on the forehead and arm for weekday, morning prayers. This is observed by Orthodox Jewish men of Bar Mitzvah age and over.

How is tefillin used?	It is made up of two leather boxes, each containing part of the Shema prayer.
	The tefillah shel rosh is bound to the head with straps and the tefillah shel yad is bound to the upper arm with straps.
	It is usually worn by Orthodox males after their Bar Mitzvah on weekday mornings during prayers but not on Shabbat or at festivals. Some women, especially from Reform Judaism, are beginning to wear tefillin.
Why is tefillin significant (important)?	It obeys the mitzvah in the Torah (Deuteronomy 6:8). A prayer is said when the tefillin is in place: 'Blessed are You, Lord our God, King of the Universe, who has sanctified us with His mitzvot, and commanded us to wear tefillin.'
What does tefillin symbolise?	It is a reminder that the wearer must serve God through developing good thoughts and through acts of compassion.

Tallit

How are tallits used?	A tallit is a four-cornered garment with fringes (tzizit).
	There are two types: tallit gadol (large), which is a large garment of wool or silk worn across the back, often called a prayer shawl. The tallit katan (small) is worn under everyday clothes with the tzizit hanging down at the corners.
	Many Orthodox and some Reform Jews will wear the tallit gadol during prayers and worship. The tallit katan is worn by some Orthodox Jews throughout the day.
Why are tallits significant (important)?	Wearing the tzizit relates to the duty to wear fringes in the corner of clothes (Numbers 15 in the Torah).
	They are often worn for worship in the synagogue.
What do tallits symbolise?	Wearing the tzizit symbolises the duty to wear fringes in the corner of clothes (Numbers 15 in the Torah).
	The prayer said before putting on the tallit shows it is a way of keeping the duties given by God.

Kippah

How is the kippah used?	The kippah is a head covering which can be of different designs and colours.
	It can be worn from childhood.
	Some Jews choose to wear it during prayer and when in synagogue, but others wear it all the time when they are awake.
	Many male Orthodox and Reform Jews wear the kippah, but there are some Reform Jewish women who wear it.
Why are kippot significant (important)?	Many male Jews choose to wear kippot during the day as well as for worship.
What do kippot symbolise?	The exact meaning is unknown, although it is often seen as a sign of respect for God as the highest part of the head is covered. It is also seen as a symbol of Jewish identity.

> **Exam tip**
>
> The content you are learning always connects with other areas of Judaism. It is important that you can make connections and explain them in your exam answers.

> **Activity**
>
> Look at the pairs of words below and explain how they are connected. Remember there may be more than one answer.
> - Mezuzah and Tefillin
> - Brit Milah and Abrahamic Covenant
> - Bar Mitzvah and Tefillin
> - Tefillin and Shema
> - Mitzvot and Tallit

Festivals and commemorations

REVISED

For this area of study you need to know about four different Jewish festivals and commemorations. For each you need to know about the *importance* or *significance*; the *preparation* and the *celebration/commemorations*.

Yom Hashoah

Significance and importance

- Yom Hashoah commemorates the Holocaust in which more than six million Jews were murdered.
- It is not a religious occasion but reminds all people that such acts of discrimination should never happen again.
- It remembers those who were murdered and also those who risked their lives to support others.
- As many of those murdered during the Holocaust have no grave, Yom Hashoah is a time of memorials.
- The emphasis of the day is on remembering the past and honouring the memory of those who suffered during the Holocaust.

Preparation and commemoration

- There are no set commemorations but opportunities are given to remember and educate people about the dangers of discrimination.
- Ceremonies are often held in synagogues or community centres, with speakers who survived the Holocaust.
- During ceremonies the Kaddish prayer for the dead is recited and candles are lit.
- In Israel, a siren blasts for two minutes and traffic comes to a standstill.
- Often six candles will be lit to symbolise that more than six million Jews were murdered.

> **Exam tip**
>
> C-type questions will ask for an explanation. This could be How? Why? Where? What? etc. It helps to underline whether you are being asked to explain how, why, what and so on, as the focus of your answer will be different depending on what you are being asked.
>
> As 8 marks are awarded for this question, you should be giving at least three developed explanations which use religious language.

Exam practice

C-type questions

Toby has been asked to write an answer to a C-type question that 'explains the commemorations associated with Yom Hashoah'. He knows he will have only about eight minutes to explain his answer and will need to use key religious terms. He has decided to include the following content. He has thought of a list of six different commemorations but knows he will have time to explain three only. Which of the following list do you think he should choose and why?
- Special services in which candles are lit.
- Special services where prayers are said.
- In Israel, a siren is blasted for two minutes.
- Many different ways are used to commemorate those murdered.
- Public discussion about the dangers of discrimination.
- The kaddish prayer is recited.

In eight minutes write out an answer which includes these three points, including the following religious terms: Kaddish, synagogues, Holocaust.

Answers online ONLINE

Rosh Hashanah

Significance and importance
- Many consider Rosh Hashanah as the day God created the world.
- Rosh means head or beginning.
- It is a happy time to celebrate the beginning of a new world.
- It is also a serious time to remember how God made the world and acts as a judge.
- Rosh Hashanah and Yom Kippur are connected in a process of judgement as many believe that on Rosh Hashanah God judges people for the deeds in the past year.

Preparation and celebration
- Special services are held in the synagogue on the eve of Rosh Hashanah.
- Special foods such as pomegranates, apples and honey will be eaten to symbolise a sweet new year ahead.
- At the morning service, a shofar (ram's horn) is blown 100 times to represent the crying of the soul asking to be reunited with God.
- Some Jews will perform tashlikh, when they cast away the crumbs in their pockets to symbolise their sins being cast away.
- During the next ten days Jews consider their deeds in the past year and try to apologise to anyone to whom they have done wrong.

Yom Kippur

Significance and importance
- Yom Kippur is often called the Day of Atonement.
- It is the holiest day of the year.
- It is the end of the ten days of repentance.
- It is a day of self-denial with a fast throughout the day.
- Many people will spend the day in the synagogue.

Preparation and celebration
- Often food and money are given to help the poor.
- Some more observant Jews will visit the mikveh (pool of natural water) for a spiritual cleaning before Yom Kippur.
- During Yom Kippur, many Jews will fast for 25 hours.
- In the synagogue, the Kol Nidrei ('All vows') is sung and the story of Jonah is told. During the prayers Jews will confess their sins to God. The service ends with the reciting of the Shema.
- After nightfall, a single blast of the shofar marks the end of the service.

Pesach

Pesach is an important celebration at home. The preparation for Pesach is an important part of the first and last celebration. There should be no work done on the days of Pesach.

> **Key concept**
>
> **Pesach** is also called Passover or the Feast of Unleavened Bread. Festival commemorating the Exodus from Egypt, celebrated in the spring.

Significance and importance

- Pesach celebrates the freedom from slavery in Egypt, which was led by Moses.
- It is often called Passover as God passed over the houses of the Israelites during the final plague.
- In the Book of Exodus, God commanded that the festival should be held each year (Exodus 12:14).
- Many of the foods eaten during the festival have special meaning. Foods without leaven (grain products that can swell), such as matzah, are eaten as a remembrance that the Israelites left Egypt before the bread had time to rise.
- The celebration is often called the Festival of Freedom and prayers are said each year for people who are not free.

Preparation and celebration

- Before Pesach begins the house needs to be rid of all its chametz (foods which have grain products that can swell).
- Families often attend synagogue and then go home for a special seder meal.
- At the seder meal the table will contain a seder dish on which there will be symbolic foods (lamb's bone, roasted egg, a green vegetable to dip in salt water, bitter herbs and a paste made of apples, walnut and wine).
- At the seder meal prayers will be read from a special book called the Haggadah.
- The door will be left open and a glass of wine is left for the Prophet Elijah, whom some Jews believe will return at the end of Pesach to announce the coming of the Messiah.

> **Activity**
>
> Put the words below into the table under the festival they are associated with.
>
> | | | |
> |---|---|---|
> | Moses | New Year | Tashlikh |
> | Egypt | Day of Atonement | Fasting |
> | Seder | Kol Nidrei | Shema |
> | Seven days | Chametz | Kaddish |
> | Creation | Prophet Elijah | Shofar |
> | Haggadah | Siren blasts | Freedom |
>
> | Rosh Hashanah | Yom Kippur | Yom Hashoah | Pesach |
> |---|---|---|---|
> | | | | |
> | | | | |
> | | | | |
> | | | | |
> | | | | |

> **Exam tip**
>
> There are two evaluation questions in each exam paper. These are very important as each one is worth 15 marks. Look at the demands of the D-style question on page 87. To achieve high marks your response needs to do much more than explain a number of points. It needs to:
> - give a detailed analysis
> - give well-supported judgements
> - use a range of religious language and sources of authority where appropriate.

Exam practice

D-style evaluation questions

'The Magen David is the best way to show Jewish identity.' [15 marks]

Discuss this statement, showing that you have considered more than one point of view. (You must refer to religion and belief in your answer.)

It is important that you show your knowledge and understanding of Judaism in your answer. It is also important to focus on what the question is actually asking by underlining the key words.

For example, the question states 'The Magen David is the best way to show Jewish identity' – the question is not asking just about the Magen David but whether the Magen David is the 'best' way to show 'Jewish identity'. In your answer you would need to refer to the other ways of expressing Jewish identity, such as festivals, Bar and Bat Mitzvahs, items worn for worship and other symbols such as the mezuzah. Remember that an important part of the answer is **justifying why** or **why not** the Magen David is the 'best' way of expressing Jewish identity.

Write an answer to this question in 15 minutes.

Answers online

Islam: core beliefs, teachings and practices

The big picture

Below is a summary of the key questions for this study of Islam:
- What is meant by prophethood (risalah)?
- What do Muslims believe about the prophets?
- What are the Islamic beliefs about the afterlife (akhirah)?
- What are predestination, human freedom, the Day of Judgement, heaven and hell?
- How do Muslim practices express identity?
- What is the significance of features of mosques, acts of pilgrimage and styles of clothing?
- What is lesser jihad?
- Why is the ummah important?
- How and why do Muslims celebrate Id-ul-Adha, Id-ul-Fitr and the Night of Power?

> **Exam tip**
>
> You will need to be able to define the concepts – the first question (for 2 marks) in each theme asks for a definition of a concept. You will also be expected to use the concepts in answers to other questions, to show that you know and understand them. The concepts help to unlock the content of the themes within the study of Islam, helping to explain religious teachings and practices and also the varying views and opinions that believers within Islam may have.

Key concepts

Prophet is a messenger of Allah. There are 25 prophets in Islam, beginning with Adam and ending with the Prophet Muhammad.

Isa is the 24th and penultimate prophet of Islam. In Christianity he is known as Jesus. Muslims believe Isa to be a messenger of God and in no way divine. Isa is believed to have had a miraculous, fatherless birth. He was a healer of the sick and foretold the coming of the final prophet, Muhammad.

Muhammad is the final prophet of Islam, to whom the Qur'an was revealed.

Ummah means 'community' and refers to the worldwide community of Muslims who share a common religious identity.

Mosque, or 'Masjid' in Arabic, is a 'place of prostration' for Muslims; it is a communal place of worship for a Muslim community.

Hijab is often used to describe the headscarf, veil or modest dress worn by many Muslim women, who are required to cover everything except face and hands in the sight of anyone other than immediate family.

Mecca (Makkah) is Islam's holiest city, located in Saudi Arabia. Mecca is the birthplace of the Prophet Muhammad and the place where Islam originated. It is the site of the Ka'bah, Islam's most sacred shrine, and is the destination of the annual Hajj pilgrimage. Muslims pray and worship facing towards Mecca, wherever they may be in the world.

Burkha is a long, loose-fitting garment which covers the whole body from head to feet. It is worn in public by some women and is compulsory for women in some Islamic countries.

Al-Qadr is the Muslim term for 'predestination', which means Muslims believe God has set out the destiny of all living things.

Akhirah is the Muslim term for the belief in the Final Judgement and life after death.

Lesser jihad The word jihad means 'to strive'. Lesser jihad is a physical struggle or 'holy war' in defence of Islam.

Id-ul-Fitr is the celebration of breaking the fast on the day after Ramadan ends.

Beliefs and practices

REVISED

Your study of Islam is separated into two areas:
- Beliefs:
  - Prophethood (risalah – Qur'an 2:136)
  - Afterlife (akhirah).
- Practices:
  - Muslim identity and ummah
  - Festivals and commemorations

> **Exam tip**
>
> **Link between beliefs/teachings and practices**
>
> Although the chapter is divided into two sections, there are many connections between the beliefs and teachings of Muslims and the practices they observe. There are also many connections between beliefs and teachings, and themes in the religious, philosophical and ethical studies component. Relevant beliefs, texts and practices will be credited wherever they appear in your answers.

Differences matter

In your studies it is expected that you will learn about the different interpretations, attitudes and practices among Muslims. The table below will help you remember why there are different views held by people who all follow the same religion.

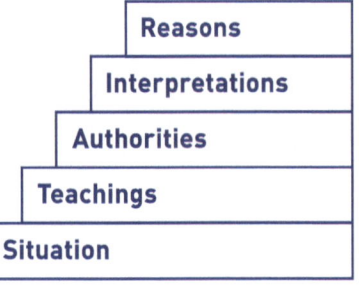

Situation	Some situations, such as daily prayer and going on pilgrimage, are important for all practising Muslims, but for other situations there may be different considerations, e.g. the importance of pilgrimage to shrines.
Teachings	The central teachings considered by Muslims would be the Qur'an. Most Muslims regard it as the revealed Word of Allah through the Angel Jibril, and most believe it contains the divine law to help people to live as good Muslims.
Authority	The Qur'an is the central source of authority for Muslims, but the Sunnah and the Hadith are also sources of authority.
Interpretation	There is no official creed in Islam, but there are slightly different interpretations of the foundations of faith between Muslims. There are connections between these two, but they have different emphases.
Reason	Islam teaches that every person has free will and that individuals will be held accountable on the Day of Judgement for decisions they have made. However, humans do have the ability to choose right from wrong and to follow the 'straight path' (Shariah) God has given. Central to Islamic belief is the idea that life is a test, and humans need to learn to turn from evil and make the right choices – this requires the use of reason and understanding of the teachings in the Qur'an and the Hadith.

> **Exam tip**
>
> Because of the many different beliefs, teachings and practices in Islam, it is important to show that you understand this diversity. When answering questions, use phrases that indicate this range: 'some Muslims …', 'often many Muslims …'

Beliefs: prophethood (risalah – Qur'an 2:136)

In this area of study you need to know about the Islamic teachings on prophethood, including Adam (the first **prophet**), Ibrahim (as the father of Ishaq (Isaac) and Ishma'il (Ishmael)), Ishma'il, **Isa** (Jesus) and **Muhammad**, as the Seal of the Prophets.

> It is important to understand that the prophets are the means through which God delivers his message to the people. They are chosen by God and the wisdom they reveal through their sayings and writings come directly from God.

> All the prophets were messengers of God, but over time the messages became lost or corrupted and so a final revelation was given through the Prophet Muhammad – the last and so the Seal of the Prophets.

Key concepts

Prophet is a messenger of Allah. There are 25 prophets in Islam, beginning with Adam and ending with the Prophet Muhammad.

Isa is the 24th and penultimate prophet of Islam. In Christianity he is known as Jesus. Muslims believe Isa to be a messenger of God and in no way divine. Isa is believed to have had a miraculous, fatherless birth. He was a healer of the sick and foretold the coming of the final prophet, Muhammad.

Muhammad is the final prophet of Islam, to whom the Qur'an was revealed.

What is prophethood?	Prophets (rusul) are humans chosen by God to receive his message on behalf of humankind.
	This channel of communication is called 'risalah'.
	The wisdom of the prophets does not come from themselves but from God.
	The Qur'an teaches that every age has been given its own prophet, bringing God's message to the people.
	Muhammad was the last prophet and is the Seal of the Prophets. Through him the will of God has been revealed fully and precisely.
Why are prophets important in Islam?	God sent many prophets throughout history to guide his people. (Qur'an 2:136 refers to 'what has been revealed to Ibrahim (Abraham) and Ishma'il (Ishmael) and Ishaq (Isaac) and Ya'qub (Jacob) and the Descendants ... and what was given to the prophets from their Lord'.)
	Prophets are human beings chosen to carry God's message.
	Twenty-five of the prophets are mentioned by name in the Qur'an. These are found in the Jewish and Christian scriptures (e.g. Ibrahim [Abraham], Musa [Moses], Dawud [David] and Isa [Jesus]).
	Muslims believe that over time the message from these prophets became lost or corrupted, so there was need for a final revelation.
	Muhammad, the Seal of the Prophets, was given the revelation of the Qur'an – God's final and absolute word.
Who are the prophets?	The four prophets Adam, Ibrahim (Abraham), Isma'il (Ishmael) and Isa (Jesus) that preceded Muhammad are important in Islamic understanding of God, communicating his message to people. Others also mentioned in the Qur'an are Nuh (Noah), Ishaq (Isaac), Yaqub (Jacob), Abdul Muttalib and Abadullah.

Islamic teachings on Adam, Ibrahim, Ishmael and Prophet Jesus

REVISED

Key concept

Isa is the 24th and penultimate prophet of Islam. In Christianity he is known as Jesus. Muslims believe Isa to be a messenger of God and in no way divine. Isa is believed to have had a miraculous, fatherless birth. He was a healer of the sick and foretold the coming of the final prophet, Muhammad.

It is important to recognise that **Isa** (Jesus) is a very important prophet in Islam – he preceded the final prophet, Muhammad. But he is seen only as a prophet of God and not as a divine being, or as the son of God.

Activity

The table below summarises Muslim beliefs about the four important prophets in Islam before the Prophet Muhammad. Learn this summary of these prophets to use in your exam answers.

Adam	Ibrahim (Abraham)	Isma'il (Ishmael)	Isa (Jesus)
Formed by God from a handful of soil; Eve (Hawwa) was created from his rib.	Born into a polytheistic family – but believed in only one God.	The second son of Ibrahim (Abraham) through Hajar (Hagar).	With Maryam (Mary), his mother, **Isa** appears prominently in the Qur'an, where it says in Qur'an 2:87 that God gave Isa 'clear proofs and supported him with the Pure Spirit'.
They lived together in paradise but disobeyed God and were banished from paradise.	Father of two sons: Ishaq (Isaac) through Sarah and Ishma'il (Ishmael) through Hajar (Hagar).	Showed exemplary faith in his father and in God – was willing to give up his life.	Given the Injil (Gospel) and performed many miracles.
Adam confessed his sin and was forgiven, becoming the first prophet.		This event is commemorated in the festival of Id-ul-Adha.	He did not die on the cross but was taken up to heaven, as God would not allow evil men to triumph over his prophet.
The father of the human race.			Isa was not God or the Son of God – only a prophet.

Exam practice

A-type questions

'What is meant by Isa?' [2 marks]

Decide which of the following answers you would award the full 2 marks and explain why.

Answer 1: Isa is Jesus.

Answer 2: Isa is the Muslim name for Jesus. He is recognised as an important prophet by Muslims.

Answer 3: Isa is one of the prophets of Islam.

Answers online

ONLINE

Exam tip

The first question in the exam will always ask for a definition of one of the concepts. To get full marks you must give an accurate definition. Ensure that you learn each of the twelve concepts carefully.

Islamic teachings on Muhammad: the Seal of the Prophets

REVISED ☐

Islamic teachings on Muhammad: a summary			
Birth	In Mecca, 570 CE. Orphaned at the age of six, brought up by his Uncle Abu Talib. Gained a reputation for truthfulness and intelligence.	**Revelation of the Qur'an**	Many further revelations of messages from God followed. These continued for 23 years (until Muhammad's death in 632 CE).
His youth	At age 20 worked for a wealthy merchant, Khadijah. Married her in 595 CE and they had four daughters and two sons (who both died). Was known as 'al-Amin' (the trustworthy one).	**Preaching**	After three years he began to preach his messages in the streets of Mecca. His main messages were: • there is one true God • we need to show thanks to God through worship • there will be a Judgement Day.
Life in Mecca	He was troubled by the corruption and cruelty in Mecca. He considered worship of idols wrong and that judgement would come.	**The Hijrah**	Many in Mecca did not accept his message. He was invited to Yathrib (Madinah) and moved there in 622 CE. This event is known as the 'Hijrah'. There he was accepted as a prophet, a political leader and a military commander.
Night of Power	He began spending much time in prayer and solitude. One night in 610 CE, while praying in a cave, he was visited by the Angel Jibril, who commanded him to recite the words that appeared. This event is known as Laylat-ul-Qadr (the Night of Power), which is mostly commemorated on the 27th day of Ramadan.	**Return to Mecca**	By 630 CE Muhammad was strongly supported. He marched with 10,000 men to Mecca and conquered the city. The Ka'bah was cleansed of idols and re-dedicated to Allah. Muhammad was now accepted as the true and final prophet of God and Islam.

The Seal of the Prophets

Muhammad is the last of the long list of prophets.

The will of Allah has been revealed fully and precisely.

There can be no more or any new prophets – Muhammad is the one who ended the series of prophets from God.

This is why he is known as the Seal of the Prophets.

Activity

Acrostics are words where the initial letter triggers the beginning of a word. They can be useful in remembering key facts about something.

Using the information in the summary, make up a simple way of remembering what Muslims mean by Muhammad as the Seal of the Prophets (page 47). Create an acrostic, like the one started below.

S

E

A

Last and final prophet

Exam practice

C-type questions

'Explain why prophets are important in Islam.' [8 marks]

Look at the band descriptors for C questions on page 86. Using the information in the section above, write an answer that merits a Band 4 mark.

Make sure you include:
- detailed explanation of the beliefs
- awareness and insight into the beliefs
- use of religious/specialist language
- sources of wisdom/authority.

Answers online

ONLINE

Exam tip

C-type questions will ask for an explanation. This could be How? Why? Where? What? etc. It helps to underline whether you are being asked to explain how, why, what and so on, as the focus of your answer will be different depending on what you are being asked.

As 8 marks are awarded for this question, you should be giving at least three developed explanations which use religious language.

Beliefs: afterlife (akhirah)

In this area of study you will need to know about Al-Qadr (predestination) and its implications for human freedom. Muslim beliefs and teachings about the afterlife, and how they relate to human freedom and accountability, are also important. You must also know about the Day of Judgement and its relationship to human freedom. Also included in this area is an understanding of Muslim beliefs about the nature, stages and purpose of heaven and the nature and purpose of hell.

Al-Qadr (predestination): implications for human freedom

REVISED

For Muslims, the will of Allah is supreme and so there is an acknowledgement that a person's life is mapped out and that the devoted follower accepts and is obedient to that calling and destiny, **Al-Qadr**.

Key concept

Al-Qadr is the Muslim term for 'predestination', which means Muslims believe God has set out the destiny of all living things.

Muslim beliefs about Al-Qadr

- God has a divine masterplan for everyone that is predestined to take place.
- This is all part of his plan for the world and all of creation.
- God knows all things in absolute detail – beyond our imagining.
- Insha'Allah ('if God is willing') is a phrase showing a believer's submission to God and his will.
- Attitudes to Al-Qadr come from the Kutub (books) of Islam.

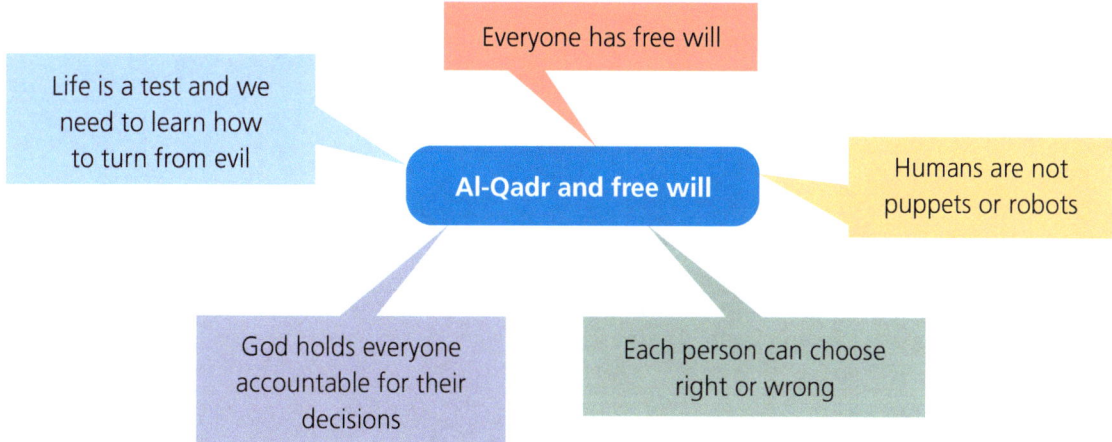

Akhirah: human responsibility and accountability

REVISED

Akhirah explains that there is a Final Judgement and this is a cornerstone of Islamic belief. The life after death that follows it is determined by the extent to which there has been obedience to the will of God and true following of his plans.

Key concept

Akhirah is the Muslim term for the belief in the Final Judgement and life after death.

Muslim beliefs about akhirah

- Every life on earth is a preparation for the eternal life to come (akhirah).
- Life is a test and all will be judged on how they have lived their lives.
- Every human has free will – they are able to make choices about beliefs and actions.
- God has given the Qur'an to help people know how to live. The Sunnah, the record of all that the Prophet Muhammad did, also helps guide Muslims to live a life that is pleasing to God.
- God will judge all people on the Day of Judgement: all will be accountable for their actions.

Human freedom and its relationship to the Day of Judgement

REVISED

Central concept: **Human freedom and its relationship to the Day of Judgement**

- The book given into the left hand shows a person will pass into hell
- The dead will be raised and stand before God for judgement
- Every human should ask themselves whether they are ready to face death and judgement
- The book given into the right hand shows a person will pass into heaven
- A book representing every action is presented to each person
- Personal intentions (niyyah) are also taken into consideration
- Good deeds and bad deeds are weighed in balance

> **Exam tip**
>
> **Making connections**
>
> In your exam you can repeat content but you must make sure it is relevant to the question. As you revise, consider your previous learning and see what connections you can make, especially to Issues of Good and Evil (Islamic Perspective) in the philosophical and ethical issues component, e.g. 'The belief in predestination (Al-Qadr) in relationship to free will', as well as in Issues in Life and Death Theme 1.

Muslim beliefs about the nature, stages and purpose of heaven (Janna)

REVISED

What will heaven be like?	It is a state of peace, joy and happiness. It will contain everything longed for on earth. It is full of beautiful gardens, sparkling fountains and flowing rivers, reclining sofas, delicious food and delightful serving maidens.
	Some also say that there are different stages or levels of heaven, from seven to even a hundred. These levels represent closeness to God: the higher the level, the closer to the Throne of God.
When will it happen?	When the dead are raised, after the sounding of the trumpet by Israfil, the two angels Munkar and Nakir will question each individual. Correct answers can be given only by those who can recite the Shahadah (statement of faith) and have also lived in submission to God and observed the Five Pillars. For those who die before the Day of Judgement, the angel of death, Azrail, takes their soul and keeps them in a state of barzakh (waiting).
What is its purpose?	Heaven is a reward for living a faithful and moral life, or for suffering persecution because of faith, or fighting in the cause for God. It separates out those who have committed a greater proportion of good deeds to bad, and whose intentions were good as well.

Muslim beliefs about the nature, stages and purpose of hell (Jahannam)

REVISED

What will hell be like?	It is a place of terror, with boiling water, fierce fire and thick black smoke. As well as physical suffering, those condemned to hell will suffer by being separated from God and having no hope of escape. Some Muslims believe it is not an eternal experience but a short period, with pardon for those who repent.
When will it happen?	After judgement, people will have to cross the very narrow Bridge of As-Sirat. Those who have collected more bad deeds and intentions than good will fall as they try to cross the bridge, so ending up in the terrors of hell. For those who die before the Day of Judgement, the angel of death, Azrail, takes their soul and keeps them in a state of barzakh (waiting).
What is its purpose?	It is a punishment for those who have failed to live faithfully and morally, and who have not ensured a sufficient weighting of good deeds and intentions. It is also thought by some Muslims to be a tool to persuade people to obey God's laws and ways because they fear the threat of going to hell. Others, however, believe most people find happiness in following the requirements of the Qur'an and learning from the example of Muhammad.

Activity

From this section on afterlife (akhirah), select important features using each of the following letters and explain the connection. Two examples have been completed.

A	
K	nowing there is a Day of Judgement should lead everyone to ask themselves if they are ready to face it.
H	
I	
R	
A	
H	ell, or Jahannam, is a punishment for those who have failed to live faithfully and morally.

Practices: Muslim identity and ummah

In this area of study you will need to know about the different ways that express Muslim identity. **Ummah** refers to the worldwide community who express their faith and beliefs in a number of ways, such as worshipping in a mosque and pilgrimage to Mecca.

Features of mosques in Wales and elsewhere

REVISED

You will need to be able to describe features of places of worship for (b) questions and be able to explain their significance or symbolism for (c) questions. For Muslims, anywhere can be a place of worship, provided it is clean. Many **mosques** adapt key features often reflecting the country of the mosque. Features have symbolic meanings.

> A mosque is a building set aside for worship, but Muslims can pray anywhere, as long as the place is clean. In some Muslim-majority countries, small areas next to a tea room or a railway station may be marked off as prayer areas. Muslims unable to get to a mosque or a place set aside for prayer at the set times for prayer will use a prayer mat and with the help of a compass will find the direction to face for their prayers.

> **Key concept**
>
> **Ummah** means 'community' and refers to the worldwide community of Muslims who share a common religious identity.

> **Key concept**
>
> **Mosque**, or 'Masjid' in Arabic, is a 'place of prostration' for Muslims; it is a communal place of worship for a Muslim community.

Architectural features of mosques

Feature	Image	Meaning or significance
Dome		Most mosques feature one or more domes.
		While not a ritual requirement like the mihrab, many say it possesses significance within the mosque – as a symbolic representation of the vault of heaven.
Minaret		A tower attached to a mosque. There may be one or a pair of minarets. The call to prayer was often made from the top of a minaret, though today it is often done using sound systems controlled from below.
		It helps to locate the mosque in a town or city.
Qibla wall		The wall in the prayer room that faces the Ka'aba in Mecca is the Qibla wall.
		It is very significant and is a requirement in all mosques. Even areas set aside for worship would have a qibla arrow.
		It is there to show worshippers which way to face when performing prayers.
Mihrab		An alcove in the qibla wall, which helps to identify the qibla wall.
		It helps to reflect the sound of the prayers back into the prayer room.
Minbar		A step of steps with a platform in the prayer room. The imam will stand on the minbar during Friday (Jumu'ah) prayers to deliver a sermon (khutbah).
		It enables the imam to be seen and heard clearly.

> **Activity**
>
> Using the information in the table, write a paragraph explaining how the features of a mosque might help worshippers.

Pilgrimage to Mecca as an obligatory act

REVISED

Pilgrimage is the fifth pillar of Islam: Hajj. The pilgrimage to **Mecca (Makkah)** is an obligatory act at least once in a lifetime for all Muslims who:
- have enough money to make the pilgrimage
- are physically and mentally fit enough for the journey and rituals.

> Because this city is the holiest and is of such importance to Muslims, non-Muslims are not permitted to enter the city at any time. To do so would spoil, even desecrate, the sacredness of the place and the spiritualness that Muslims believe it has.

What is pilgrimage to Mecca?	It is called 'Hajj' – a pilgrim completing it is known as Hajji (male) or Hajjah (female).
	It lasts five days and occurs once a year.
	Observance of Hajj is recognition of the uniqueness of God, his unity, power and wisdom.
	It is the fifth pillar of Islam (an obligatory act of most Muslims, once in a lifetime).
What is the purpose of pilgrimage to Mecca?	To visit the holiest city on Earth – the city of God.
	Ibrahim (Abraham) was commanded by God to sacrifice Isma'il (Ishmael) there.
	Ibrahim rebuilt the Ka'bah as a place of worship to the one true God.
	To remember that the Prophet Muhammad was born in Mecca and received his first revelation from God there.
	He reclaimed the city for God before his death.
What are the practices and rituals involved in the pilgrimage?	On arriving, pilgrims enter Ihram (a state of purity), dedicating themselves to humility and prayer and putting on the special plain garments of white unsewn cloth.
	During this period, pilgrims should not cut hair or nails, wear perfume or have sex.
	They circle the Ka'bah seven times, Tawaf, anticlockwise, and drink from the Zamzam well. This reminds them of Ibrahim's wife, Hajar (Hagar), who was shown the well by an angel when she was desperate for water. These take place in Mecca.
	At Mina: pilgrims spend the night and then throw pebbles at the three pillars (symbolising rejection of the devil and his temptations); sacrificing an animal (symbolising Ibrahim's willingness to sacrifice his son). This is a festival called Id-ul-Adha. Men will also shave their heads (symbolising the completion of their Hajj).
	They stand before God on the great Plain and at the Mount of Mercy at Arafat.
	Tawaf (circling the Ka'bah) – is repeated at Mecca.

Key concept

Mecca (Makkah) is Islam's holiest city, located in Saudi Arabia. Mecca is the birthplace of the Prophet Muhammad and the place where Islam originated. It is the site of the Ka'aba, Islam's most sacred shrine, and is the destination of the annual Hajj pilgrimage. Muslims pray and worship facing towards Mecca, wherever they may be in the world.

Exam tip

In B questions you will be required to describe beliefs, teachings or practices. Each response should take about five minutes. To gain full marks, you are required to write 'an excellent, **coherent description** showing **awareness and insight** into the religious ideas, belief, practice, teaching or concept. Uses **a range of** appropriate **religious/specialist language** and terms and, where relevant, sources of wisdom and authority, **extensively**, **accurately**, **and appropriately**.' The key words are highlighted for you.

Exam practice

B-type questions

Below you will find a typical B question. Form your answer using the information and guidance on this page. You have about five minutes to complete your answer.

Describe how Muslims prepare for pilgrimage. [5 marks]

ONLINE

Clothing: hijab, niqab and burkha

REVISED ☐

Muslims will wear clothing that reflects their culture and interpretations of passages from the Qu'ran. Many believe it is important that clothing is modest and does not excite sexual interest.

For men this means covering the main parts of their bodies; for many women, especially in traditional Muslim countries, it means long dresses and **hijab** (headscarves).

> Muslim society places a high value on the need for people to dress in a responsible way. This applies to both men and women, though often the focus is on women ensuring that, when in public, no flesh is exposed, other than face, hands and feet. Some Muslim women prefer to wear hijab when going out – they feel it is a sign of both their gender and their religion.

> The **burkha**, a total covering garment, is more common in very traditional Muslim communities or countries, such as Afghanistan. In some countries, not wearing the burkha when going out depends on the culture of the country or of individual families; however, some women choose to wear it even when they may not be required to do so.

Key concept

Hijab is often used to describe the headscarf, veil or modest dress worn by many Muslim women, who are required to cover everything except face and hands in the sight of anyone other than immediate family.

Key concept

Burkha is a long, loose-fitting garment which covers the whole body from head to feet. It is worn in public by some women and is compulsory for women in some Islamic countries.

Exam tip

'D' evaluation questions

There are two evaluation questions in each exam paper. These are very important as each one is worth 15 marks. Look at the demands of the D question on page 87. To achieve high marks your response needs to do much more than explain a number of points.

For 12–15 marks:
- An excellent, **highly detailed analysis** and evaluation of the issue based on **comprehensive and accurate knowledge** of religion, religious teaching and moral reasoning.
- Clear and **well-supported judgements** are formulated and a **comprehensive range of different and/or alternative viewpoints** is considered. Uses and interprets religious/specialist language, terms and sources of wisdom and authority **extensively, accurately, appropriately and in detail**.

> **Exam practice**
>
> Below are some aspects to consider including in an answer to the following question:
>
> Muslim dress customs are out of date. [15 marks]
>
> Discuss this statement, showing that you have considered more than one point of view. (You must refer to religion and belief in your answer.)
>
> In your answer, make sure you have:
> - selected alternative or different viewpoints
> - shown how belief influences individuals, communities and societies
> - formed judgements
> - taken no longer than fifteen minutes to write your response.
>
> Use and explain the following, in the light of the guidance in the exam tip on page 54, to formulate a complete answer:
> - Dress customs are more cultural than religious.
> - Dress customs help to create a religious identity, which is important for many people today.
> - Freedom of religious expression is important in society today, so people should be allowed to wear whatever they want.
> - Dress customs to create a sense of modesty are important even now.
> - Some countries, such as France, have banned the wearing of the burkha in public, and some people agree with this ban because they say that the burkha oppresses women and belongs to the past.
>
> **Answers online** ONLINE

Lesser jihad

Jihad is a much misused term. There are two types of jihad:
- The way in which a believer struggles every day to live as a good Muslim – following the rules and practices required of them (this is the greater jihad).
- The expectation that a Muslim may have to stand up for their religion and defend it when in a country or place where the religion is not accepted or commonly practised (this is the **lesser jihad**).

In your answers, make sure you refer either to the greater jihad or to the lesser jihad.

> This concept arose during the Prophet Muhammad's lifetime, when he gave his faithful followers authorisation to fight. The Qur'an (2:190) makes it clear that it should be in defence only and that means defending Islam and Islamic values, strengthening Islam, righting a wrong, defending the right to practise Islam or defending Muslims from attack.

Key concept

Lesser jihad The word jihad means 'to strive'. Lesser jihad is a physical struggle or 'holy war' in defence of Islam.

The lesser jihad

- The lesser jihad is the use of force only in self-defence, sometimes called the holy war, and is the removing of evil from society.
- It originates from Muhammad's decision to authorise taking up conflict to prevent the wiping out of Muslims and is supported in the Qur'an (22:39: 'Permission [to fight] has been given to those who are being fought, because they were wronged').
- The Qur'an 2:190 also states: 'Fight in the way of Allah those who fight you but do not transgress.'
- Muslims should not attack first; aggressiveness is forbidden. Muslims should fight only those who attack, and should never kill civilians.
- Jihad can be declared only by a holy and pure Muslim leader whose decision is supported by the whole Muslim community.

The Qur'an also lays down strict conditions for a war to be called a jihad as shown in the acrostic below:

Come to an end as soon as the enemy surrenders

Opponents must have started it

No fighting for land gain

Do not rape or abuse women

Innocent people should not be killed or hurt, nor property damaged

The last resort: all other peaceful ways must have been tried

It is designed to bring about good

Only a religious leader can authorise it

No poisoning of water should be done

Soldiers who are wounded should be treated equally and with respect, whichever side they are from.

Practices: festivals and commemorations

In this area of study you will need to know about how Muslims, in Wales and elsewhere, celebrate the festivals of Id-ul-Adha and Id-ul-Fitr, and how the giving of the Qur'an on the Night of Power is commemorated.

Id-ul-Adha

REVISED

What is it?
- Id-ul-Adha is the festival of sacrifice.
- It is the most important festival in Islam.
- It is sometimes called 'the Greater Id'.
- It marks the end of the annual Hajj (pilgrimage).
- It is the opportunity for Muslims across the world to worship together.
- It is a commemoration of the example and commitment of Ibrahim.
- It underlines the importance of personal sacrifice in terms of commitment to God.

How is it celebrated?
- Preparations include gifts being bought, new clothes made, food prepared, arrangements made for the sacrifice of an animal.
- It is a public holiday in some countries: Indonesia, Turkey, Jordan.
- In Wales and the rest of the UK, some Muslim organisations or businesses may close during Id-ul-Adha. Some children may have the day off school.
- Prayers will be said in the mosque and an Id prayer heard.
- Friends and relatives will be visited, wearing new clothes.
- Traditionally, each Muslim family will buy and sacrifice an animal. In Wales and the rest of the UK, Muslims may ask a butcher to slaughter a sheep for them and then share it in a communal meal.
- It is a sacred duty to give some of the meat from the animal to the poor.

> **Activity**
> Make a summary list of the key activities done during Id-ul-Adha.

Id-ul-Fitr

REVISED

> **Id-ul-Fitr** is the name for the joyful three-day celebration which takes place at the end of Ramadan. It is a reward for the completion of the month of fasting and a time to give God thanks for the strength and self-control experienced during the time of fasting.

> **Key concept**
> **Id-ul-Fitr** is the celebration of breaking the fast on the day after Ramadan ends.

What is it?
- Id-ul-Fitr is the festival of breaking fast after Ramadan.
- There are three days of joyful celebrating at the end of Ramadan.
- It is a reward for the completing and ending of the fast period.
- It is a thanksgiving to God for giving Muslims strength and self-control during Ramadan.

How is it celebrated?

- It is a public holiday in Muslim-majority countries. In Wales and elsewhere in the UK, some Muslim businesses will close for the period of the festival. The Welsh government advises schools they may authorise absence for Muslim students on the day it is celebrated.
- Houses will be decorated with coloured lights, banners and flags.
- New clothes will be bought and worn.
- Prayers will be said and a sermon listened to in the mosque.
- 'Id Mubarak' (Happy Id) will be said and cards sent.
- Families and friends will be visited and special meals prepared together and shared.
- Many Muslims will go to cemeteries to remember and pay respect to family members who have died.
- Gifts and money will be given to children.
- Gifts of charity will be given to the poor – Zakat-ul-Fitr.
- In some countries there are specific customs: fish recipes (Egypt), egg fights for men (Afghanistan), henna designs on hands and feet for women (India).

> **Exam tip**
>
> **'B' type questions**
>
> Part 1 B questions usually require a description of a religious idea, belief, practice, teaching or concept. The band descriptors (see page 85) give clear guidance on what is required, and the top band (Band 3, 4–5 marks) expects 'an *excellent*, *coherent* description, showing *awareness* and *insight*'. It also states that a 'range of appropriate religious/specialist language and terms' is used. In addition, it says 'where relevant, sources of wisdom and authority' should be used 'extensively, accurate and appropriately'.

> **Activity**
>
> Write three sentences to describe the celebrations that end fasting for Muslims.

The Night of Power

What is it?
- The Night of Power is one of the holiest days in the Muslim calendar – the 27th day of Ramadan.
- It marks the date when the Qur'an was revealed to the Prophet Muhammad.

How is it celebrated?
- Many Muslims stay up all night reciting from the Qur'an.
- They pray and remember God's mercy and forgiveness.
- They take time off work to do extra worship (ibadah).
- They commit time to study and recite the Qur'an in greater depth, thinking deeply about the meaning of the passages.

The importance of the revelation of the Qur'an
- The Qur'an is the divine law, sent by God to guide humans in the right way to live.
- It was revealed to the Prophet Muhammad by God through the Angel Jibril.
- It was written down in Arabic by the Prophet Muhammad's followers and put into one book shortly after the Prophet Muhammad's death (623 CE).
- Before using the Qur'an, Muslims will be in a state of wudu and a suitable frame of mind.
- When it is being read, the Qur'an is often placed on a wooden stand.
- When not in use, it is wrapped in a cloth and stored on the highest shelf.

REVISED

Islam: core beliefs, teachings and practices

Activity

Sort the words below into the table, matching up which word is associated with which festival.

Revelation of the Qur'an

27th day of Ramadan

Coloured flags and banners

End of Ramadan

Visiting cemeteries and lights

End of Hajj

Angel Jibril

Commemorate the commitment of Ibrahim

Id-ul-Adha	Id-ul-Fitr	Night of Power

Theme 1: Issues of relationships

The big picture

Below is a summary of the key questions to think about for this theme:
- What is the nature of relationships?
- Why are there different attitudes to adultery and divorce?
- What is the nature and purpose of sex?
- How are the nature and purpose of marriage expressed through marriage ceremonies?
- Should divorced individuals be allowed to remarry in places of worship?
- Should same-sex marriages be allowed in a place of worship?
- Do men and women have equal roles in leading worship?

Issues of relationships   REVISED

Your study is divided into three areas:

Relationships

Beliefs attitudes and teaching about the nature and purpose of relationships in the twenty-first century: families; roles of women and men; marriage outside the religious tradition; cohabitation; the nature and purpose of marriage as expressed through marriage ceremonies; adultery and divorce.

Sexual relationships

Teachings and attitudes about the nature and purpose of sex, the use of contraception and same-sex relationships.

Issues of equality: gender prejudice and discrimination

Attitudes towards the roles of women and men in worship and authority.

For all three areas, make sure you know sufficient detail from two different religions or religious traditions about these three areas.

> **Key concepts**
>
> **Adultery** is voluntary sexual intercourse between a married person and a person who is not their spouse.
>
>  **Divorce** is to legally end a marriage.
>
> **Cohabitation** is to live together in a sexual relationship without being married or in a civil partnership.
>
> **Commitment** is a sense of dedication and obligation to someone or something.
>
> **Contraception** is methods used to prevent a woman from becoming pregnant during or following sexual intercourse, e.g. artificial or natural.
>
>  **Gender equality** is when people of all genders enjoy the same rights and opportunities in all aspects of their lives.
>
> **Responsibilities** are actions or duties you are expected to carry out, such as looking after family members.
>
>  **Roles** are the position, status or function of a person in society, e.g. a police officer, as well as the characteristics expected of them, e.g. to obey the law.

Questions about relationships

REVISED ☐

- Do our roles change with age or circumstances?
- Does it matter where same-sex weddings take place?
- Are families important in the twenty-first century?
- Would it matter if someone married a person from a different religion?
- What difference does marriage make?
- Why do different religions have different marriage ceremonies?
- What and why do religions teach about contraception?
- Do men and women have the same roles and responsibilities during worship?

> **Activity**
>
> **Use of command terms**
>
> In the exam paper you will be asked four questions from this unit. Each of the questions will have different demands. In the chart below the meaning column has become jumbled. From the command word try to identify which would be the correct meaning.
>
> | Command | Meaning |
> |---|---|
> | What is meant by … [2 marks] | Evaluation of a view from more than one perspective. These perspectives can all be 'for' the statement, all be 'against' the statement or be a mixture of both 'for' and 'against', e.g. 'Sex outside marriage is always wrong.' Discuss this statement showing that you have considered more than one point of view. (You must refer to religion and belief in your answer.) |
> | Describe … [5 marks] | Definition of a key term (linked to one of the key terms identified for each unit), e.g. 'What is meant by roles?' |
> | Explain … [8 marks] | Demonstrate knowledge and understanding by describing a belief, teaching, practice, event, etc., e.g. Describe religious teachings about inter-faith marriage. |
> | Discuss this statement showing that you have considered more than one point of view (you must refer to religion and belief in your answer). [15 marks] | Demonstrate knowledge and understanding of a topic by explaining the statements made with reasoning and/or evidence, e.g.:
 • Explain how …
 • Explain why …
 • Explain the main features of …
 • Explain the importance/significance of …

 e.g. 'Explain from Christianity and another religion you have studied attitudes to divorce.' |

> **Exam tip**
>
> You will often need to answer questions from two religious traditions and to show different viewpoints within each tradition. It is important that you know the content of each religion you are studying. If unsure you can find the details on www.wjec.co.uk/qualifications/religious-studies/gcse.

Theme 1: Issues of relationships

Relationships

In this area of study you will be looking at the nature and purpose of different types of relationships, including families and marriage. You will also need to explain different religious attitudes to issues such as **roles** of women and men, divorce and adultery. For each religion you are studying you will be expected to know specific religious practices and teachings.

Key concepts

Roles are the position of a person, e.g. a police officer, as well as the characteristics expected of them, e.g. to obey the law.

Responsibilities are actions/duties you are expected to carry out, such as looking after family members.

Within any family there will be different roles played by each family member. In some religious traditions there are specific roles expected of the mother and father in supporting children's religious understanding and practice. In the twenty-first century there will be many differences in roles between families of the same religion. This often depends on social influences such as which parent is working. With each role comes **responsibilities** that family members have. Sometimes these will be influenced by religious teachings.

REVISED

Key religious teachings on the nature and purpose of families

Christianity

- The family is an important place for the nurture and celebration of faith. Pope Francis described it as 'the essential cell of society'.
- It is important to worship together as a family at home and at church.
- It is important to celebrate festivals such as Christmas and Easter as a family.
- It is important to mark special times in family members' lives such as baptism and confirmation.
- Mothers and fathers are expected to play an equally important role in family life although they may have different responsibilities.
- In the Ten Commandments children are expected to honour their parents. This can be interpreted as obeying them but also caring for them when they are old.
- Children are often considered as gifts from God.

Islam

- Mothers and fathers are expected to play an equally important role in family life, although they may have different responsibilities.
- The family often includes the extended family of parents, grandparents, uncles and aunts.
- The role of the family honour is important.
- It is considered important to celebrate festivals at home together, e.g. Id-ul-Fitr.
- It is considered important to keep the halal diet together at home.
- Children are expected to care for their parents and older family members.

Judaism

- Mothers and fathers are expected to play an equally important role in family life although they may have different responsibilities, e.g. on Shabbat women light the candles to bring Shabbat into the home and fathers bless the children.
- Jewish values and practices are central to family and home life, e.g. keeping kashrut.
- In the Ten Commandments children are expected to honour their parents. This can be interpreted as obeying them but also caring for them when they are old.
- It is considered important to celebrate festivals together at home, such as Pesach.

> **Exam tip**
>
> **Answering B-type questions**
>
> In B-type questions you will be required to describe beliefs, teachings or practices. Each response should take about five minutes. To gain full marks you are required to write 'an excellent, **coherent** answer showing **awareness** and **insight** into the religious idea, belief, practice, teaching or concept. Use a range of **religious/specialist language, terms and sources of wisdom and authority** extensively, accurately and appropriately.' The key words are highlighted for you.

Exam practice

Below you will find a typical B-type question and some points that could be included in a response. Select three of the bulleted points that are most important and form these three points into a paragraph that answers the question. Include specific language or teachings from the religions you have studied. And remember – you only have five minutes.

Describe ways in which families are important in a faith community.
- Reference to the expectation of family units in religious teachings
- Reference to the functions of specific types of family, e.g. the distinctive role of members in an extended family
- Unit established for support and care
- Celebrate important religious festivals together
- Keep the practices of a religion
- Expectation of religious/non–religious beliefs that within a family there will be specific duties for members
- Care of the elderly and young.

Use a table like the one below to make your own notes.

Points to make (choose three from list above)	Religious teachings and language to support the point chosen

Answers online

ONLINE

Theme 1: Issues of relationships

The nature and purpose of marriage

REVISED

Marriage ceremonies celebrate the importance of marriage, and contain rituals and symbols that reflect the nature and purpose of marriage. Throughout marriage ceremonies the importance of **commitment** is emphasised.

> Partners show in public their commitment to each other during a marriage ceremony. This might be through ritual action or spoken or written words.

Key concept

Commitment is a sense of dedication and obligation to someone or something.

Exam tip

Questions might ask about 'marriages outside the religious tradition.' Answers could include marriage between two different groups within the same religion, e.g. Sunni and Shi'a Muslims or Roman Catholic and Quaker traditions. It could also include marriage between someone who belongs to a religious tradition and someone who is an atheist or humanist.

Marriage outside religious traditions

In a pluralistic society, two people of different faiths may wish to marry. Look at the diagram below, and consider the issues raised by each of the circles – be sure you can explain what these are and the pressures they will place on the marriage.

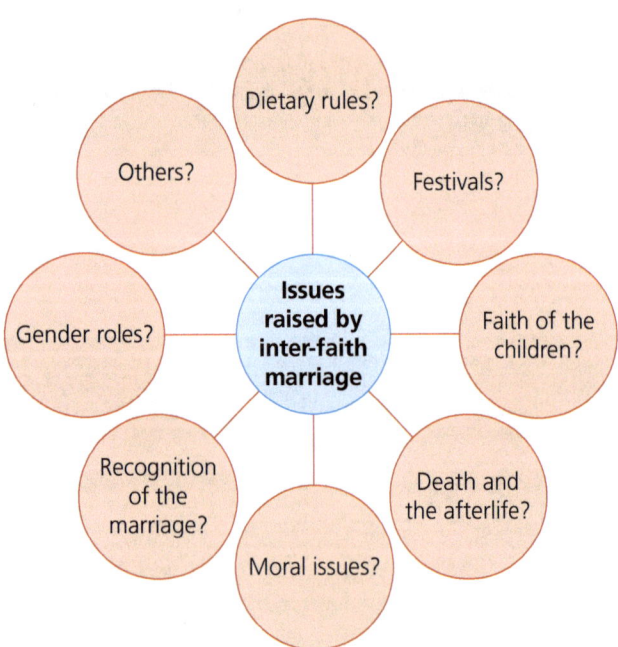

Exam tip

In C-type questions you might be asked to explain the main practices or teachings from two different religions or religious traditions. Take care not to just describe ceremonies, but to make clear the nature and purpose of marriage that they celebrate.

Key religious teachings on the nature and purpose of marriage

REVISED

Christianity

Marriage is:
- a sacrament in some traditions (e.g. Catholic). Ceremonies are often held in a church or chapel performed by a vicar or minister
- marriage is God's intention as referred to in the New Testament (Mark 10:6–8)
- the vows taken in a marriage ceremony (e.g. 'in sickness and in health') show lifelong commitment.
- the exchange of rings represents eternal love.

Judaism

Marriage is:
- a blessing from God
- an important spiritual ceremony
  - seven blessings are said praising God for creation and happiness
  - the groom places an uncut ring on the bride's index finger – a symbol of eternity
  - the groom stamps on a wine glass – a symbol of the fragility of marriage (or for some a reminder of the destruction of the temple in Jerusalem)
- the basis of family life. The couple stand under the *chuppah* – representing the Jewish home – and the *ketubah* (contract) is given to the bride, stating the care of the husband for his wife.

Islam

Marriage is:
- a gift from Allah. Qur'an 30:21 refers to God creating a soul mate for humans to have
- the basis of family life. Many Muslim families will assist in the finding of a bride or groom. The *nikkah* takes place in a mosque or the bride's home, to demonstrate the marriage is under Islamic law (for Shia Muslims, the *nikkah* must have six verses read publicly), and the marriage contract is signed with witnesses, symbolising the commitment and undertaking of the couple
- in Wales and England, the *nikkah* is not a legally recognised marriage. In order to be legally married, the couple must also undergo a civil ceremony
- the need to have a companion. The *wali* (woman's guardian) offers the bride to the groom, to symbolise the groom's responsibility for his wife.

Exam tip

In a C-type question you need to write about two different religions or religious traditions. It might be that the two traditions you are studying have lots of similarities as well as differences. Mention this in your exam answer.

Cohabitation and adultery

REVISED

In the examination you may be asked questions on religious beliefs, attitudes and teachings about **cohabitation** and **adultery**. The key religious teachings are shown below, but it is important to remember that there will be different views and practices between believers in the same tradition.

> Being faithful to your partner is important in all religious traditions. Promises and commitments are made during marriage ceremonies, which are often held in sacred or holy places of worship.

> There are many different views regarding cohabitation between and within religious traditions. Often views regarding cohabitation will depend upon the couple's commitment to each other.

Key concepts

Adultery is voluntary sexual intercourse between a married person and a person who is not their spouse.

Cohabitation is to live together in a sexual relationship without being married or in a civil partnership.

Exam practice

Roles is one of the key concepts in this unit. Below are some responses to an A-type question. If you were an examiner, which would you give 2 marks to and why? Look at the marking information on page 85 to help you.

Question
What is meant by roles?

Possible answers
1. What you do.
2. The way a person lives out their responsibilities (e.g. mothers and children).
3. How you show that you act out your duty as a husband or wife.

Answers online

ONLINE

Key religious teachings on cohabitation

REVISED

Christianity
- Sexual relationships are considered sacred and special so, traditionally, cohabitation and adultery were prohibited.
- Some Anglicans do accept cohabitation in committed relationships.
- The Catholic Church and some Anglicans do not accept cohabitation.
- Some Baptist churches refuse to marry couples who are cohabiting.

Judaism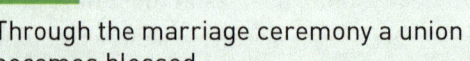
- Through the marriage ceremony a union becomes blessed.
- Living together does not express or show the same commitment as marriage.

Islam
- Sexual relationships should take place within marriage.
- Cohabitation is generally regarded as wrong.
- In practice, some Muslims will choose to cohabit.

Answers at www.hoddereducation.co.uk/myrevisionnotesdownloads

Key religious teachings on adultery

REVISED

Christianity

- Marriage is sexually exclusive and a sacrament (gift from God), so adultery is unacceptable.
- Adultery breaks the vows made at the wedding.
- The Ten Commandments forbid it (Exodus 20:13).
- Adultery spoils the special relationship between a married couple.
- Adultery may harm the family unit.

Islam

- Sex outside of marriage is disapproved of so adultery is unacceptable.
- During the marriage ceremony, vows promising faithfulness are exchanged.
- Adultery can be harmful socially, so goes against the unity and peace of the ummah.
- Surah 17:32 describes adultery as a shameful thing, opening the way to other evils.

Judaism

- The Ten Commandments specifically forbid adultery (Exodus 20:13).
- *Halakhah* (code of conduct) excludes extramarital sex, as the husband should be sexually considerate towards his wife.
- Marriage is a union sanctified (*kiddushim*) by heaven, so it is within that state that men and women are most fulfilled.

> **Exam tip**
>
> If you can refer to relevant sources of wisdom or sacred texts to support your answer it will help you get high marks. You don't need to remember the exact words or references, but state in your own words what they say and how believers interpret them.

Divorce, separation and remarriage

REVISED

You will need to know different attitudes between and within religions concerning **divorce** (and annulment), separation and remarriage.

> There are many different attitudes to divorce within religious traditions. In the twenty-first century many religious traditions are reconsidering their attitudes to the status of divorced men and women, and considering issues such as. Is remarriage allowed? and Can people remarry in a place of worship?

Key concept

 Divorce is to legally end a marriage.

Key religious teachings: divorce and remarriage

REVISED

Most religions and religious traditions expect marriage to be a lifelong commitment, but they also accept that sometimes a relationship reaches a point where the only solution is to end it. Four terms are important to be clear about:
- divorce: the legal ending of a marriage
- separation: the couple deciding to live separately
- annulment: the 'cancelling' of a marriage (in the Catholic Church)
- remarriage: when a person who has been married wishes to marry someone else.

> **Exam tip**
>
> Often marks are lost because candidates write generally about an area. Divorce is not the same as remarriage, and religions have different attitudes and teachings on each.

Christianity

- Divorce is accepted as a legal ending of marriage, but is discouraged (Mark 10:9).
- Every effort at reconciliation should be made.
- Remarriage is discouraged, but when chosen, a non-church wedding is expected in some denominations.
- Ministers are free to choose whether to conduct a remarriage service.
- Jesus' teaching in Matthew 19:9 regards remarriage after anything other than unfaithfulness as committing adultery.
- Jesus stated (Mark 10:9) that no one should separate what God had joined (in marriage).

The Catholic Church:
- Marriage is a lifelong commitment that only ends at death.
- Marriage is a sacrament and cannot be dissolved.
- A civil divorce may be allowed, but remarriage is not then possible.
- An annulment is available where there is complete breakdown, however, if an annulment takes place, remarriage is possible.

Islam

- Divorce is allowed as a last resort. Before a couple divorces, they should be helped to be reconciled (Qur'an 4:35).
- A period of three months (the *iddah*) of trying to be reconciled must be taken first.
- If divorce does take place, the wife receives the final part of her dowry and should be treated well (Qur'an 2:229).
- Remarriage is allowed, as there is no concept of celibacy in Islam.
- In the Qur'an (4:128–130) it is made clear that it is not wrong to separate if they both agree.

Judaism

- Divorce is a last resort.
- Both a religious and civil divorce are needed for Orthodox Jews.
- In Orthodox Judaism, the husband must give his wife a 'get' (document of divorce)
- Reform Jews accept a civil divorce, although some rabbis encourage the obtaining of a get.
- Remarriage is often encouraged as the Torah refers to remarriage after the death of a partner.
- Remarriage is possible after 90 days, following the receiving of a get for Orthodox Jews.
- In Deuteronomy (24:1–4) a man is forbidden to remarry a wife he had divorced and who had married another man, even if this second husband died; this would really be seen as going against Exodus 20:14: 'Do not commit adultery.'

> **Activity**
>
> Select three points for each of the religions you are studying which explain attitudes to divorce and remarriage.

Sexual relationships

In the examination you will be asked questions that will require you to know the religious teachings about the nature and purpose of sex and the use of **contraception**.

> Often religious teachings are considered in order to reach ideas on contraception. There may be many different views and attitudes within the same religious tradition depending upon the interpretation of the religious teachings.

You will also need to know different attitudes to same-sex relationships and to recognise there are different attitudes within the same religious tradition. You will need to be able to describe varying teachings and interpretations from two religions or religious traditions.

Key concept

Contraception is methods used to prevent a woman from becoming pregnant during or following sexual intercourse, e.g. artificial or natural.

Key religious teachings: sex and contraception

REVISED

Christianity

- Sex should take place within a committed relationship such as marriage.
- Sex is holy and sacred, and a gift from God.
- Sexual relationships are special and unique and a commitment between husband and wife.
- Casual sex is seen as devaluing people.
- Sex outside of marriage (adultery) is harmful to the special relationship of marriage.
- Contraceptives are acceptable to many Christians as long as both partners agree.

For Catholics:
- Artificial methods of contraception are not allowed – it's against the Natural Law (St Thomas Aquinas).
- Sex should always allow the possibility of new life (because of the second of Aquinas' five primary precepts).
- Natural methods of contraception are allowed, such as natural family planning.
- Priests are expected to be celibate.

Islam

- Sex should only take place within marriage (unlawful sexual intercourse is immoral, Qur'an 17:32).
- Sex is considered an act of worship.
- Sex is one of the ways of meeting a partner's needs.
- Use of contraceptives is acceptable where both partners agree.
- Contraceptives that potentially harm the body or are more permanent (such as sterilisation) are generally not acceptable.

Judaism

- Sex is one of three stages of marriage: betrothal (the promise), contract (the wedding), consummation (sex).
- Having children is believed to be part of God's will.
- Use of contraceptives is permissible if both husband and wife agree.
- Orthodox Jews consider natural methods of contraception as the only acceptable ones.
- Reform Jews allow most forms of contraception to limit family size.
- Sex outside of marriage (adultery) is prohibited by the Ten Commandments, as well as the Halakhah, which emphasises a husband's need to be sexually considerate to his wife.

Exam practice

D-type evaluation questions

Below is an evaluation question and a list of possible viewpoints. Identify four viewpoints that you think are the strongest. Add evidence to support the views and complete your response to the question.

Cohabitation is always wrong. [15 marks].

Discuss this statement showing that you have considered more than one point of view. (You must refer to religion and belief in your answer.)
- Marriage shows a committed relationship as vows are made to each other.
- Many religions teach that sex should only be a part of a committed marital relationship.
- People should have free will to form whatever relationships they want as long as they do no harm.
- Some people cannot marry as it is too expensive.
- Some people cohabit before taking any vows or making commitments.
- There are many different forms of contraception.
- Adultery can cause distress in a family.
- A ring and certificate do not prove there is a loving relationship.

You can use the table below to make your own notes.

Points to make (choose four from list above)	Religious teachings and language to support the point chosen

Answers online

> **Exam tip**
>
> **Evaluation**
>
> The D-type questions always ask you to discuss the statement. In your answer you need to consider other views. These views might all be in support of the argument or all against the argument or some for and some against. What is important is that they are different. Your answer gives you a chance to apply what you have learnt from the rest of the unit.

Key religious teachings: same-sex relationships

Christianity

- Many Christians oppose same-sex relationships and marriages on biblical grounds, and tend to regard marriage as between a man and a woman (Leviticus 20:13 refers to same-sex relations as 'a disgusting thing' punishable by death; 1 Timothy 1:8–10 explains that laws are made for those who do wrong, including those who take part in same-sex activities).
- Anglicans currently do not allow same-sex marriages in church, though some clergy might agree to a church blessing.
- Quakers have welcomed same-sex marriages for some years.
- The United Reformed Church has allowed individual churches to have same-sex marriages in their buildings if they wish to.
- Catholics prohibit same-sex marriages as they see marriage as a union between a man and a woman.

Islam

- Sex should only take place between a husband and wife.
- Same-sex marriages or relationships are not allowed (Qur'an 7:80–81).

Judaism

- Interpretations of the Torah, for example, Leviticus 18:22, result in different attitudes and practices.
- Orthodox Jews do not allow same-sex marriages, although some may accept same-sex relationships.
- Reform Jews often support same-sex marriages.

Issues of equality: gender prejudice and discrimination

In this section you will be asked questions about the roles that men and women play within the religious tradition and about gender prejudice and discrimination.

> **Key concept**
>
>  **Gender equality** is people of all genders enjoying the same rights and opportunities in all aspects of their lives.

There are different traditions between and within religions regarding the role of women in worship and authority.

Roles of women and men: in worship and authority   REVISED

Christianity

- The original disciples were all men.
- Jesus had women followers.
- 1 Timothy 2:11–12 can be interpreted to say women should not have authority over men.
- Galatians 3:27–29 can be interpreted to say gender is not important as long as there is faith in Jesus.
- Roles of men and women are taught as equally important but might be different.
- Anglicans now allow women to be ordained and become bishops.

Catholics:
- Women can have an active role, for example, nuns helping to lead worship.
- Women cannot be ordained.
- Pope Francis has emphasised the important role that women play in the church.

The Church in Wales:
- Women are allowed to be ordained as priests and become bishops.

Anglican:
- Women are now allowed to be ordained and become priests.
- In 2014, the first female bishop in the UK was ordained.

Judaism

- Some of the mitzvot do not apply to women, for example, wearing tefillin.
- There are different attitudes within as well as between Reform and Orthodox Judaism.
- The bringing in of Shabbat to the home is conducted by women.
- Roles of men and women are taught as equally important but might be different.

Orthodox:
- In the UK only men are allowed to be rabbis.
- Men and women sit in different parts of the synagogue.
- Only men can form the minyan (a group of ten men over the age of thirteen).

Reform:
- There are female and male rabbis.
- Men and women sit together in the synagogue.
- Women may wear tallit and kippah in the synagogue if they wish.

Islam

- Teachings such as Qur'an 4.1 show Allah created all people from the same soul.
- In the Qur'an someone who is a true believer can be male or female (Qur'an 40.40).
- The Qur'an suggests that men should have authority over women in situations such as divorce (Qur'an 2.228).
- Usually it is only men who take on the roles of imam and lead prayer for men and women.
- Men and women are usually separate for worship.
- Some Sunni groups allow women to lead prayers for other women but they must stand within the congregation.
- Roles of men and women are taught as equally important but might be different.

Activity

Look at the pairs of words below and explain how they are connected. Remember, there may be more than one answer.
- Commitment; Adultery
- Sex; Marriage
- Equality; Discrimination
- Families; Faith

Theme 2: Issues of human rights

The big picture

Below is a summary of the key questions to think about for this theme:

- Why is human life special?
- How do religious people support human rights?
- What happens when personal conviction and the law conflicts?
- What do religions teach about prejudice and discrimination?
- Should people always have the right to express their views?
- How do religious people work to tackle poverty?
- Are some forms of poverty worse than others?
- How should wealth be used?

Issues of human rights

REVISED

Your study is divided into three areas:

Human rights and social justice

Beliefs, teachings, practices and attitudes about the dignity of human life, examples of conflict between personal conviction and the laws of the country, censorship and freedom of expression.

Prejudice and discrimination

Beliefs, teachings and attitudes towards prejudice (including racial prejudice) and discrimination.

Issues of wealth and poverty

Considerations concerning acquisition and use of wealth and the actions and attitudes of religious charities.

For all three areas, make sure you know sufficient detail from two different religions or religious traditions about these three areas.

Key concepts

 Censorship is the practice of suppressing and limiting access to materials considered to be obscene, offensive or a threat to security. People may also be restricted in their speech by censorship laws.

 **Discrimination** is treating groups of people or individuals differently, based on prejudice.

 Extremism is believing in and supporting ideas that are very far from what most people consider correct or reasonable.

 **Human rights** are the basic entitlements of all human beings, afforded to them simply because they are human.

 Personal conviction is something a person strongly feels or believes in.

 Prejudice is pre-judging; judging people to be inferior or superior without cause.

 Relative poverty is a standard of poverty measured in relation to the standards of a society in which a person lives, for example, living on less than a certain percentage of average UK income.

 **Absolute poverty** is an acute state of deprivation, whereby a person cannot access the most basic of human needs.

 Social justice is promoting a fair society by challenging injustice and valuing diversity. Ensuring that everyone has equal access to provisions, equal opportunities and rights.

Human rights and social justice

In this area you will be looking at teaching and attitudes toward the dignity of human life and practices used by religious traditions to promote **human rights**. You will consider where there have been conflicts between personal conviction and the laws of a country and the role of censorship, freedom of expression and extremism.

> Religious and non-religious believers consider human rights as an entitlement for all people. In many religious traditions teachings from sacred texts and the examples of founders and leaders give direction to how believers should promote human rights.

> **Social justice** involves realising that injustices exist and if not checked will grow and widen; and learning how to promote equality while encouraging and celebrating diversity. It also involves understanding that rights also carry responsibilities.

Religious believers, individually and collectively, are involved in campaigns for promoting human rights and social justice. For many, their commitment is influenced by a belief in the dignity of all human life.

Key concepts

Human rights are the basic entitlements of all human beings, afforded to them simply because they are human.

Social justice is promoting a fair society by challenging injustice and valuing diversity. Ensuring that everyone has equal access to provisions, equal opportunities and rights.

Exam practice

Command terms

In the exam paper you will be asked four questions from this unit. Each of the questions will have different demands. In the chart below the meaning column has become jumbled.

From the command word try to identify which would be the correct meaning.

Command	Meaning
What is meant by … [2 marks]	Evaluation of a view from more than one perspective. These perspectives can all be 'for' the statement, all be 'against' the statement or be a mixture of both 'for' and 'against', e.g. 'It's important for all people to work for social justice.' Discuss this statement showing that you have considered more than one point of view. (You must refer to religion and belief in your answer.)
Describe … [5 marks]	Definition of a key term (linked to one of the key terms identified for each unit), e.g. 'What is meant by social justice?'
Explain … [8 marks]	Demonstrate knowledge and understanding by describing a belief, teaching, practice, event, etc., e.g. Describe religious teaching about respect for others.
Discuss this statement showing that you have considered more than one point of view. (You must refer to religion and belief in your answer.) [15 marks]	Demonstrate knowledge and understanding of a topic by explaining the statements made with reasoning and/or evidence e.g.: • Explain how … • Explain why … • Explain the main features of … • Explain the importance/significance of … e.g. 'From Christianity and another religion explain attitudes towards obeying the law.'

Answers online

ONLINE

Key religious teachings on the dignity of human life

REVISED

Christianity

- Belief that all humans are created in the image of God (Genesis 1: 26–27).
- Jesus showed in his teachings and practice all life should be valued and treated with respect, e.g. visiting the lepers, Parable of the Good Samaritan.
- Teachings from Pope Francis in Evangeli Gaudium refers to the importance of caring for the homeless and elderly.
- Every person is sacred and of worth is a core Christian belief.
- Each person should be treated with selfless, unconditional love – agapé.

Islam

- The Qur'an refers to the uniqueness of each individual and the importance of helping just even one individual (Qur'an 5.32).
- Allah created all life and therefore it should be treated with respect.
- Importance of the worldwide community of Muslims – ummah – in which all are equal.

Judaism

- Belief that all humans are created in the image of God (Genesis 1: 26–27).
- Teachings from the Talmud regarding the actions of humankind should be like those of God.
- A belief that insulting another human is like insulting God.
- Importance of all Jews to perform tzedekah (charity and justice) to other human beings.

Activity

Making connections

Many of these beliefs and teachings can be used in answers to questions from other areas of philosophy and ethics. For the two religions you are studying, identify teachings and beliefs that could answer on:
- capital punishment
- abortion.
- euthanasia.

Religious practices to promote human rights, including equality

REVISED

Christianity

Agape in action

Following the action of Jesus many Christian charities express agapé, e.g. helping at Salvation Army hostels; working in church food banks; volunteering for St Vincent de Paul.

Islam

Ummah in action

The ummah promotes welfare of the Muslim community, e.g. paying of zakat and sadaqah to help the poor; volunteering for charities such as Islamic Relief.

Judaism

Tzedekah in action

Through tzedekah Jews should practise charity giving and promoting social justice, e.g. performing mitzvot for others, fundraising and volunteering for charities such as Tzedek.

Conflict between personal convictions and the laws of a country

REVISED

Often a person's beliefs or **convictions** influence their actions. There have been many times when the beliefs of someone conflict with the actions of others or the law of a country. When this happens religious believers will often pray and read sacred texts for guidance. They will also consider how the leaders and founders of their religion acted.

Key concept

Personal conviction is something a person strongly feels or believes in.

Exam practice

In your exam you may be asked to describe how someone's personal conviction has conflicted with the law. In your answer you could describe one particular belief, for example, the right to wear the hijab or the right to euthanasia. Or the actions of one particular person who has acted on their beliefs to oppose a law, for example, Martin Luther King Jr. There will be many examples you have studied that you can refer to.

Fill in the chart like the one below by adding an appropriate quote or comment where there is a blank.

Issue	Personal conviction	Law of the country	Action
Race equality	All people should be treated equally as all are made in the image of God.	In America people were segregated with separate schools, seating areas on buses, etc.	Martin Luther King led non-violent action, e.g. protest marches, made speeches, etc.
Abortion	The belief that all life is created by God and is sacred.	Many countries such as Britain allow abortions under certain conditions.	Some religious believers campaign outside abortion clinics, write letters of protest and pray for changes in the law.
Same-sex marriages	That marriage is between a man and a woman, and not members of the same sex or gender.	Many countries do allow marriage of same-sex partners.	Some believers protest against such marriages, and write letters or hold placards outside places where a same-sex marriage is being conducted.
The right to euthanasia		The law in Britain does not allow euthanasia or assisted suicide.	Some people campaign for the law to be changed, using the courts, protests and writing letters.
Capital punishment		Capital punishment is no longer used in Britain.	Some people hold campaigns and vigils, and write letters asking that capital punishment be reintroduced.

Answers online

ONLINE

Censorship, freedom of expression and religious extremism

REVISED

There is a difficult balance between **censorship** and freedom of expression. People hold many different views and beliefs and sometimes these can conflict with others.

Extremist beliefs are often formed through personal interpretations of sacred texts. It is sometimes believed that particular actions will please a divine being and result in a better afterlife. There are many examples of religious **extremism** but they all share a belief that they are acting on a personal conviction.

> I should be allowed to say and do what I want.

> Even if it offends me and goes against my religious beliefs?

Key concepts

Censorship is the practice of suppressing and limiting access to materials considered to be obscene, offensive or a threat to security. People may also be restricted in their speech by censorship laws.

Extremism is believing in and supporting ideas that are very far from what most people consider correct or reasonable.

In Britain and many countries in Europe, everyone is free to express their ideas and feelings or reactions about religious, political, economic or government matters. This reflects Article 19 of the United Nations Declaration of Human Rights, which states that everyone has the right to freedom of opinion and expression. Likewise, Article 9 of the European Convention on Human Rights upholds freedom of thought, conscience and religion. However, there are laws in many countries that require people to refrain from inciting violence and discrimination in expressing their views, and to also be careful to not offend others either, as that is against other laws. Some of these laws are rules of censorship, whereby the publication or broadcasting of certain types of material is prohibited.

Often, when it comes to freedom of religious expression, it can be difficult to decide where one person's freedom to express and demonstrate their belief or religious faith becomes an offensive or derogatory matter to another person who has different beliefs or faith. This is particularly so for religions that contain within their beliefs the need or desire to share that personal faith with others. Trying to agree exactly when and how 'witnessing' to others about your own faith and explaining it or promoting it to others is acceptable and when it is not can be very difficult.

This is where extremism has become an important concept and issue, for it begins to identify what is most commonly considered as beyond reasonableness. To religious extremists, their beliefs and actions are just and moral, and even a duty; yet to others, even in their own country or their own religion, their views, and especially their actions, are considered unacceptable and untenable.

Although it is difficult to get total agreement, it is agreed that some of the main characteristics of extremism include:
- **absolutism**: there is no alternative to what is believed or stated, which is seen as right
- **heroic leadership**: extremists often follow a charismatic leader who incites passionate allegiance, especially from young idealists, and who recount stories of great achievements
- **immovableness**: extremists are usually unwilling to consider any compromise; their own position is believed to be the only possibility
- **narrow-mindedness**: most extremist causes have one focus and one goal; all else is irrelevant
- **superiority**: their view and belief is the ultimate, and their cause the greatest, to the extent that others can be demeaned and dehumanised for their failure to see the truth
- **sacrifice**: extremist groups tend to expect their followers to be willing to sacrifice anything and everything, including their own or their family's lives, in the greater good of the cause.

> ### Activity
>
> In this unit of study you have come across many concepts and throughout your exam you will be expected to use a wide range of religious and specialist terms. It is important that you are able to use these with precision and make connections with other specialist terms.
>
> Explain the links between the following:
> 1. Dignity of life *and* social justice
> 2. Personal conviction *and* extremism
> 3. Human rights *and* personal dignity
> 4. Human rights *and* freedom of expression
> 5. Freedom of expression *and* censorship

There is a difference between prejudice and discrimination.

Prejudice is when a person is judged without any evidence. All religions agree that people should treat others as they want to be treated. (Prejudice is the thought.)

Discrimination is treating people differently because of their race, gender, religion or class. Religious believers would say it is wrong as everyone is part of a divine creation. (Discrimination is the action.)

Prejudice and discrimination

In this area of study you will learn about the beliefs, attitudes and teachings about **prejudice** and **discrimination** from the two religious traditions you have studied. You will need to know about the specific actions and attitudes of a religious person or religious charity.

> **Key concepts**
>
>  **Prejudice** is pre-judging; judging people to be inferior or superior without cause.
>
>  **Discrimination** is treating groups of people or individuals differently, based on prejudice.

Prejudice is to do with our thoughts, what we think.

Whereas discrimination is the actions or behaviour that arises from those thoughts which results in people being treated unfairly and unjustly.

Beliefs, teachings and attitudes towards prejudice and discrimination

REVISED

Christianity

- Prejudice and discrimination are unacceptable, and are against Christian beliefs and teaching.
- God created all human beings as equals, whatever race, ability or gender (Galatians 3:28).
- The Ten Commandments give guidance on living in harmony with others.
- Jesus' example (such as his treatment of lepers and outcasts) and his teachings (such as the Good Samaritan).
- Jesus did not discriminate against women (e.g. John 4 where Jesus asked a Samaritan woman for a drink of water).
- The Roman Catholic and Greek Orthodox churches do not allow women to become priests.
- In many other churches, such as Anglican or Methodist, women can be priests, ministers or bishops.

Judaism

- All humanity is made in the image of God, and all have the same responsibility towards God.
- Being a 'chosen' nation is not being above others, but having additional responsibilities and duties.
- Israel accepts Jews from all nations and races.
- In the Mishnah it is taught that the bond between human beings is so great that doing harm to one person is like doing harm to the whole world (Mishnah Sanhedrib 4.5b).
- Women take an important role in religious ceremonies in the home, and Jewish identity is established through the female line.
- In some branches of Judaism, such as Reform or Liberal Judaism, women can become rabbis.
- In Orthodox synagogues, women sit in a separate part of the synagogue.

Islam

- All people are equal, though not the same (Qur'an 49:13).
- All people are important in their own right, as created by Allah; men and women both face the same judgement.
- The ummah (brotherhood) crosses all national, cultural, political, racial and language boundaries.
- The act of prayer stresses the importance of equality: individuals stand as equals before Allah; and in pilgrimage, all pilgrims wear the same white ihram clothing.
- Muhammad respected women and selected Bilal, the black slave, as the first muezzin.
- Qur'an 5:8 teaches that men and women have equal religious and ethical rights.
- Women are allowed particular rights and protections (to have no sexual harassment; to be cared for in pain or difficult times; to be provided for; to wear the hijab (satr) for keeping modesty).

Attitudes towards racial discrimination and examples of campaigners

REVISED

Christianity

Martin Luther King Jr

- As a Christian he believed in Jesus' teaching on love and non-violence, and that all humans were equal in the eyes of God.
- He believed in and dreamed of a world where people would not be discriminated against because of their race, but would be equal citizens.
- He gave speeches, organised campaigns and protest marches – all of which were peaceful and non-violent – to promote equality for all.
- He said: 'We must learn to live together as brothers or perish together as fools.'
- He said: 'Mankind must evolve for all human conflict a method which rejects revenge, aggression and retaliation. The foundation of such a method is love.'

Islam

The Christian Muslim Forum

- It is based in London and brings together Christians and Muslims so as to build good relationships.
- It creates safe places for discussion and exploration of differences between Christianity and Islam.
- It educates others through inter–faith dialogue and activities, for communities, students and teachers, women, young people and international development agencies (especially those working in Africa and Iran).

Judaism

JCORE (Jewish Council for Racial Equality)

- It believes concern for social justice should be an important part of Jewish identity.
- It runs activities and campaigns to try to combat racism.
- It has a Muslim Jewish taskforce that works together to tackle race hate.
- It organises JUMP, which is a befriending project for unaccompanied asylum-seeking children and young people.
- It has a refugee doctors mentoring scheme, to help refugee doctors requalify in the UK.

Exam practice

An example of a D-type question is:

It is important for all people to work for social justice. [15 marks]

Discuss this statement showing that you have considered more than one point of view. (You must refer to religion and belief in your answer.)

In answer to this question a candidate has decided to include points from the following areas of the unit. For each point add further details and write a paragraph for each that could be used in the answer.

Point	Details to include	Paragraph
Many sacred texts refer to the importance of working for social justice		
Many people work for social justice as a practical expression of their belief in the dignity of God's creation		
Religious leaders have stressed the importance of working for social justice to create a more just society		
Some people believe that religion and politics should not be connected		

Exam tip

The D-type questions always ask you to discuss a statement. In your answer you need to consider other views. These views might all be in support of the argument or all against the argument or some for and some against. What is important is that they are different. Your answer gives you a chance to apply what you have learnt from the rest of the unit.

Answers online ONLINE

Issues of wealth and poverty

In this area of study you will consider the acquisition and use of wealth. You will focus on the actions and attitudes of a charity of each of the religions you have studied.

> **Exam tip**
>
> It is important that you can identify the differences between the acquisition and use of wealth. Questions may be asked on the acquisition or the use or both.

The acquisition of wealth

This means the ways in which people become rich or wealthy, by:
- being paid for work, especially if it is a high salary job, such as a sports star, or TV presenter
- running their own business; some grow rapidly and become valuable
- inheritance, from a relative who has died
- criminal activity, such as fraud or burglary
- gambling in its various forms.

The use of wealth

This is about how people use their money and wealth. For many people, it is a mix of:
- buying material things (a place to live, food, possessions and accessories)
- paying for holidays and travel
- giving to charities
- helping family and friends
- investing, for future needs.

The idea of **relative poverty** involves understanding the criteria by which assessments of people's lives are made, and the extent to which there are many who fall below the basic levels; and learning how to support those who are in such need.

Absolute poverty describes the situation of many thousands of people in the world. People living in absolute poverty simply do not have the necessary means to support themselves or their families. If we accept this fact, it is possible to challenge systems and processes that either lead to their acute needs, or which do not enable them to be helped out of them.

> **Exam tip**
>
> Often marks are lost because candidates write generally about an area. Acquisition of wealth is not the same as use of wealth, and religions have different attitudes and teachings to the two; make sure you know these clearly.

Key concepts

Relative poverty is a standard of poverty measured in relation to the standards of a society in which a person lives, for example, living on less than a certain percentage of average UK income.

Absolute poverty is an acute state of deprivation, whereby a person cannot access the most basic of human needs.

Ethical considerations about the acquisition and use of wealth

Christianity

- Spiritual values are the most important.
- A person's value should be based on their actions rather than their possessions.
- Being wealthy is not bad or wrong; it depends how the wealth was acquired.
- Many Christians oppose gambling, particularly Methodists and Quakers, because it encourages greed or the love of money for its own sake.
- Most Christians believe giving to charities and those in need is an important part of their faith. Some give a tenth of their income (a tithe) to good causes.

The Parable of the Rich Man and Lazarus (Luke 16:19–31) warns of putting great store by riches:

- The rich man, who had everything in life, and paid no attention to the poverty and needs of Lazarus who sat at his gates, died.
- He suffered a hell in the afterlife as he had only ever thought about physical pleasures.
- Lazarus, who had suffered physically in life, went to heaven and enjoyed a new life there.

Islam

Proper use of one's wealth is of lasting value.
- All wealth is a gift from Allah.
- It is not wrong to be wealthy; the wealthier you are the more generous you should be.
- Wealth should not be used to harm others.
- Islam promotes four types of giving:
  - zakat (Sunni and Shi'a): 2.5 per cent of wealth every year, for the poor and needy
  - khums (Shi'a) 20 per cent of savings, paid to Muslim scholars and leaders for community welfare
  - sadaqah (all Muslims): any good deed done out of compassion to generosity (of time or money)
  - zakat-ul-fitr: donation at the end of Ramadan, for the poor (so even those in poverty can eat a generous meal at Id-ul-Fitr).

'[True] righteousness is [in] one who believes in Allah … and gives wealth … to relatives, orphans, the needy, the traveler, those who ask [for help], and for freeing slaves … and gives zakat.' (Qur'an 2:177)

Judaism

- Giving to those in need is a duty.
- All possessions belong to God, so should not be chased after nor rejected.
- People should budget carefully so as to provide for families.
- Pushkes (collecting boxes) are encouraged, as is tithing (giving a tenth).
- Wealth should be used for the benefit of the community.

Jewish philosopher Maimonides identified eight levels of charity:
1. Giving a little but not willingly.
2. Giving but only a little when someone has a lot.
3. Giving to a person after being asked.
4. Giving to a person face to face but before being asked.
5. Giving without knowing to whom, but with the recipient knowing who the giver is.
6. Giving anonymously but knowing who the recipient is.
7. Giving anonymously and not knowing who the recipient is.
8. Finding employment for someone.

Actions and attitudes of religious charities to alleviate poverty

REVISED

Christianity

Christian Aid

Attitudes:
- aims to challenge systems that favour the rich
- reflects a belief that God loves all and the dignity of all human life
- committed to being effective stewards of the planet's resources.

Actions:
- organises projects to educate people
- runs campaigns and Fairtrade activities
- works cooperatively with faith and secular groups
- publicises examples of inequality and poverty.

Christianity

Food banks

Attitudes:
- expresses Christian values by sharing food, following Jesus' instructions in the Sermon on the Mount
- puts into practice Jesus' teachings of giving to those in need, e.g. 'When I was hungry you gave me something to eat' (Matthew 25:35–36).

Actions:
- organised by many churches individually or with other places of worship, to help people within the local community
- food is donated, sorted and stored by the local worshipping community and then given to food bank clients who are in need
- volunteers often meet with clients and signpost them to other agencies which support with housing needs, etc.

Judaism

Tzedek

Attitudes:
- reflects Jewish attitudes of loving the stranger
- believes it's important to work across religious and racial boundaries.

Actions:
- organises projects to educate people
- runs campaigns and raises awareness of social injustice
- publicises examples of inequality and poverty.

Islam

Islamic Relief

Attitudes:
- guided by Muslim values to create a caring world
- aims to show compassion, justice and sincerity through their actions.

Actions:
- responds to disasters and emergencies
- provides long-term support for shelter and education
- supports orphans financially and emotionally.

Exam tip

In your exam you might be asked to write about a charity for each of the religions you are studying. It is important to remember that the charity must be one from a religion. Marks will not be awarded for general descriptions of the charity, but for information about the actions and attitudes of the charity.

Activity

Consider three points for each of the two traditions you have studied that are distinctive.

Name of religion	Acquisition of wealth	Use of wealth

Marking grids

Answering the questions

It is important to know the structure of the exam paper and the type of questions that will be asked.

For all exam questions consider two questions:
- **How** many marks are awarded for the question? This will help you consider how much time should be spent on your answer and the depth of your answer.
- **What** is the question asking you to do? No question will ever ask you to write all that you know! What are the most important words in the question? Remember you can highlight them to help you focus on what the question is asking.

It is important to remember that there are **four types** of questions. Each has the maximum number of marks after the question. The space in your exam booklet will give you an idea of how much to write. It is also important to look at the marking grids so you can see what is required for each of the mark bands.

Question (a)

- 1 mark for each relevant point made.
- 2 marks for either two separate points or one point which is developed/explained/elaborated.

These are always the first question in each unit. They ask you to explain what the key concept means. Your explanation can include an example.

Remember there are only 2 marks available for these questions, so it important you are able to give an accurate definition which is to the point.

Question (b)

In these questions you will be expected to describe a particular religious teaching or view. There is a maximum of 5 marks for this type of question. To gain full marks you should be able to show your **knowledge** using appropriate **religious terms** and any **relevant sources of wisdom or sacred texts**.

Band	Band descriptor	Mark total
3	An excellent, coherent description showing awareness and insight into the religious idea, belief, practice, teaching or concept. Uses a range of appropriate religious/specialist language and terms and, where relevant, sources of wisdom and authority, extensively, accurately and appropriately.	4–5
2	A good, generally accurate answer showing knowledge and understanding of the religious idea, belief, practice, teaching or concept. Uses religious/specialist language and terms and, where relevant, sources of wisdom and authority generally accurately.	2–3
1	A limited statement of information about the religious idea, belief, practice, teaching or concept. Uses religious/specialist language and terms and, where relevant, sources of wisdom and authority in a limited way.	1
0	No relevant information provided.	0

Question (c)

These questions expect you to 'explain' a key practice, belief or issue in the religions you have studied. There is a maximum of 8 marks for this type of question. You need to use appropriate religious terms and relevant sources of wisdom or sacred texts.

Band	Band descriptor	Mark total
4	An excellent, highly detailed explanation showing awareness and insight into the religious idea, belief, practice, teaching or concept. Uses a range of religious/specialist language, terms and sources of wisdom and authority extensively, accurately and appropriately.	7–8
3	A very good explanation showing awareness of the religious idea, belief, practice, teaching or concept. Uses a range of religious/specialist language, terms and sources of wisdom and authority accurately and appropriately.	5–6
2	A satisfactory explanation showing some awareness of the religious idea, belief, practice, teaching or concept. Uses religious/specialist language, terms and/or sources of wisdom and authority with some accuracy.	3–4
1	A limited explanation showing little awareness of the religious idea, belief, practice, teaching or concept. Uses religious/specialist language, terms and/or sources of wisdom and authority in a limited way and with little accuracy.	1–2
0	No relevant information provided.	0

Answers at www.hoddereducation.co.uk/myrevisionnotesdownloads

Question (d)

These are very important questions as they are worth 15 marks. The question requires you to read and understand a statement and then:

Discuss this statement showing that you have considered more than one point of view. (You must refer to religion and belief in your answer.) (15)

Band	Band descriptor	Mark total
4	An excellent, highly detailed analysis and evaluation of the issue based on comprehensive and accurate knowledge of religion, religious teaching and moral reasoning. Clear and well supported judgements are formulated and a comprehensive range of different and/or alternative viewpoints are considered. Uses and interprets religious/specialist language, terms and sources of wisdom and authority extensively, accurately, appropriately and in detail.	12–15
3	A very good, detailed analysis and evaluation of the issue based on thorough and accurate knowledge of religion, religious teaching and moral reasoning. Judgements are formulated with support and a balanced range of different and/or alternative viewpoints are considered. Uses and interprets religious/specialist language, terms and sources of wisdom and authority accurately, appropriately and in detail.	8–11
2	A satisfactory analysis and evaluation of the issue based on some accurate knowledge of religion, religious teaching and moral reasoning. Some judgements are formulated and some different and/or alternative viewpoints are considered. Uses and interprets some religious/specialist language, terms and/or sources of wisdom and authority with some accuracy.	4–7
1	A weak analysis and evaluation of the issue based on limited and/or inaccurate knowledge of religion, religious teaching and/or moral reasoning. A limited and/or poor attempt or no attempt to formulate judgements or offer different and/or alternative viewpoints. Poor use or no use of religious/specialist language, terms and/or sources of wisdom and authority.	1–3
0	No relevant point of view stated.	0

Question d will also have 6 marks available for spelling, punctuation and the accurate use of grammar.

Notes